My Time At The Box
A Memoir

2017
Special First Edition

Written By
Nathan Denny

My time at the box

Nathan Denny

MY TIME AT THE BOX

Part memoir &.
Part historical recollection.

73-75 Pershore Street

NATHAN DENNY

BLURB INC

First published in Great Britain in 2017

First published by Nathan Denny

First printed by
Blurb Inc
580 California St Ste 300. San Francisco,
CA 94104-1024.

This first edition printed and bound in the United States of America by Blurb Inc.

http://dnathan2.wixsite.com/dennywriting

10 9 8 7 6 5 4 3 2 1

CONTENTS

CONTENTS

To the box,
Our box,
Our glorious box,
Why oh why did they bury you, our box?

- Author, Nathan Denny

AUTHOR'S NOTE

An unmeasurable weight is lifted from my shoulders as I type this because henceforth I acknowledge that I'm done, we're done, it's over. Everything I've had to say, wanted to say and felt like I've needed to say for such a long time is laid out in plain English in the countless number of pages beyond this one. I thank you for a very memorable part of my life and every single thing that came as a result of it but I respond in regret that it's long since been over and I'm sorry that we've had to go through all this again, both the good and the bad, but it's been necessary to ensure that the memories are preserved. Even if this book is only printed and purchased once by myself through a self publishing company and sits on my bookshelf for the remainder of time I've still done it. I've achieved something I set out to achieve all that time ago and have since moulded everything you see before you form nothing but scraps of paper, memory and time.

While the stories only just beginning for you, Reader, I ask you to acknowledge that for me writing this it's over. I thank you for joining me on the journey that you're only just about to embark on and hope every chapter proves its worth in regards to the time that it takes you to read through them all.

I hereby wish everyone that features in this story, and those of whom played a part but do not, all the very best for their future.

- Author, Nathan Denny

My time at the box

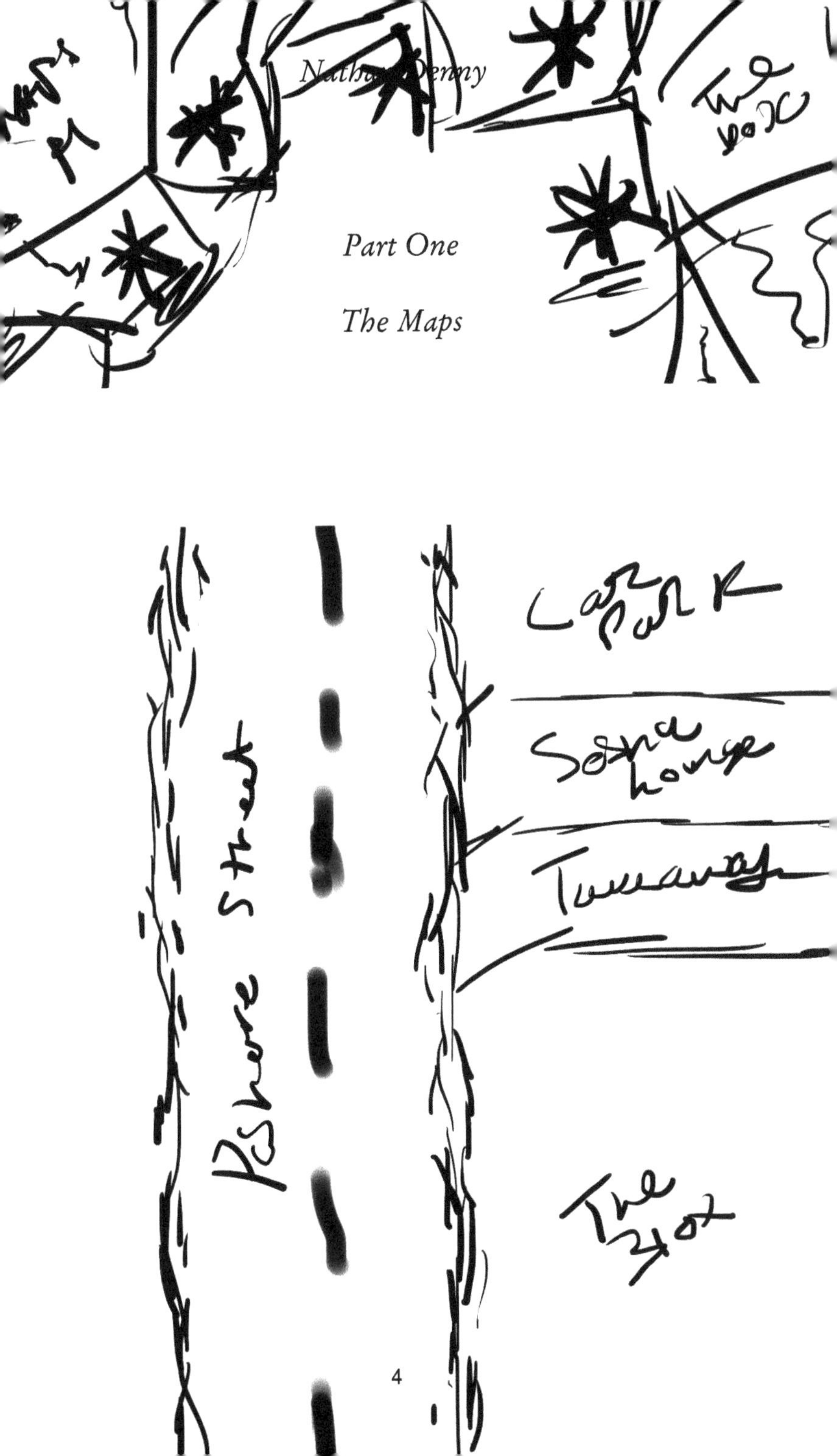

Part One

The Maps

THE MAPS

Such is the vast content that I have compiled over the three years of writing this manuscript (2014-2017) or the five years of living it (2012-2017) that I feel that perhaps for all the depth that the manuscript will entail it is important, from the outset, that the reader, you, are able to follow the events than hereon I will describe in all their entirety. I feel it important because while I, the writer, know all the events inside and out, because I have lived through them, perhaps someone whom may obtain this title, an outsider, will not and therefore I hope only that if along the way you are diverted from the path of the manuscript and find yourself wondering that the pages, and maps, that follow this are able to guide you on painting a visual image, if such material is needed, in order to be able to follow the manuscript as well as I or anyone else of whom features in the story that follows could.

I ask you, Reader, to understand that the maps that follow are to be used as a visual guide only and that expectations should be not be placed upon that are higher than is due. In summary the maps have been created based on nothing but memory and therefore imperfections will be present. Imperfections can range from the missing of details altogether to things in the wrong place to objects appearing on a grander or smaller scale than was true. I ask the reader to understand, on the scale note, that I have done, to the best of my ability, my designs as such that I believe things to be in the correct place. Errors such as things appearing a different shape to what they actually were may also appear, although again I believe not to be the case since my memory is all I can believe. I have included name tags of all the important parts on the maps that follow to further enrich the readers knowledge of The Leisurebox and it's ins-and-outs of the design of the place. Furthermore I ask the reader to understand that the maps that follow are of the building as it stood in 2012-2014 and next to nothing changed in design throughout that period. Any errors that are present, or things that I feel need explaining, are written in their appropriate length and location.

Image to the right shows 73-75 Pershore Street, Birmingham in 1952 prior to the construction of the ice rink and bowling alley in 1964-1965.

The area of what would later become 73-75 Pershore Street, on the map, is shown as the area inside the marked arrows.

The map can be found at Birmingham Library Archives (located on floor number 4). The map reference number is SP 0786 SW

The next record of the map that they hold is 1970-1971 and therefore, at the time of writing, falls under the 50 year crown copyright law and is unable to be used for anything other than personal viewing. A copy can be purchased (a A4 photocopy) but a declaration must be signed before such material can be obtained. To obtain a copy of the 1970-1971 map ask for a ticket at the main desk on floor 4 and use the above reference number so the staff member may obtain the exact map for you.

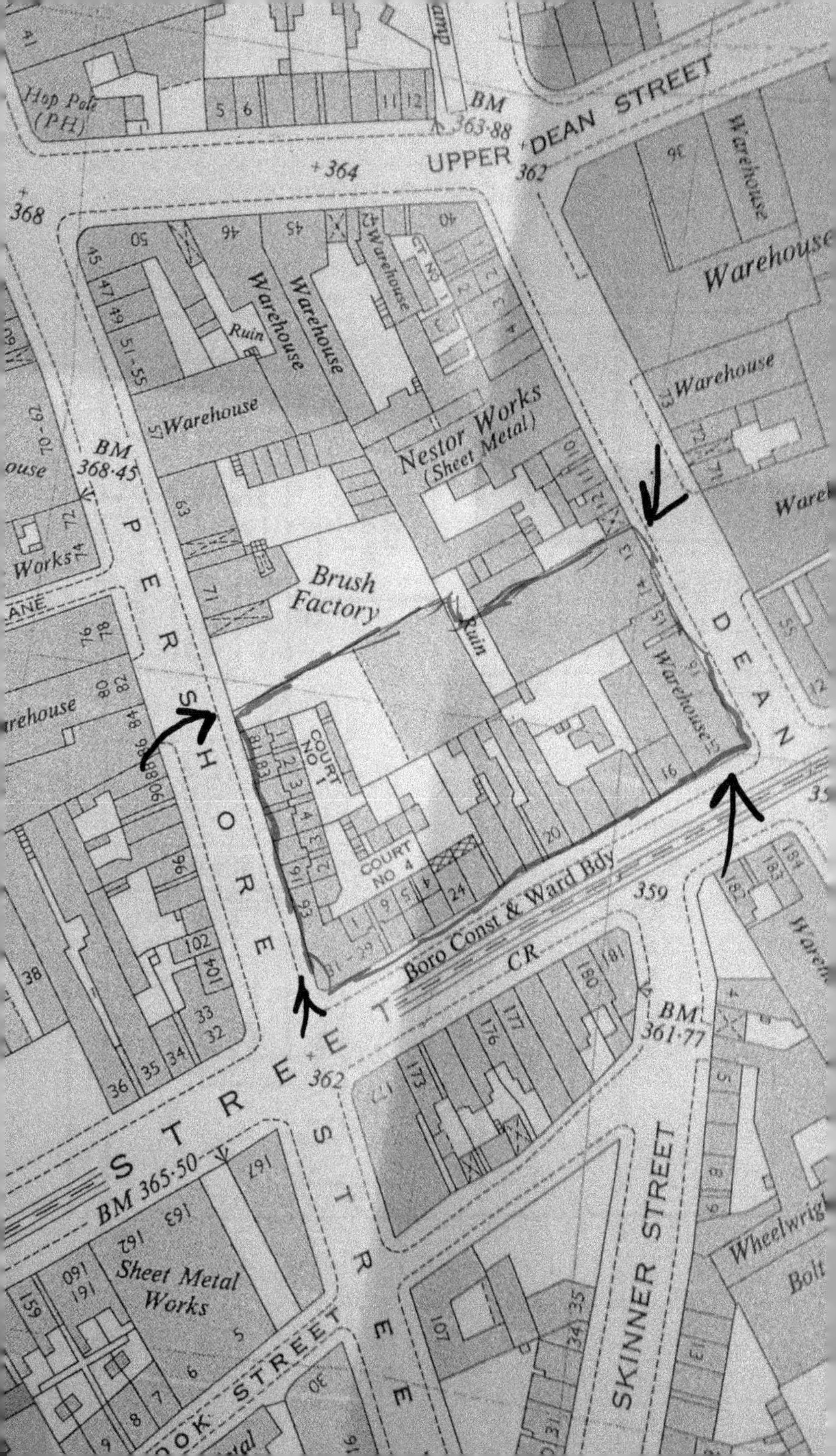

UPPER DEAN STREET
Hop Pole (PH)
BM 363·88
Warehouse
Ruin
Nestor Works (Sheet Metal)
Brush Factory
Court No 1
Court No 4
Boro Const & Ward Bdy
BM 368·45
BM 361·77
BM 365·50
DEAN
UPPER SHORE STREET
SKINNER STREET
Sheet Metal Works
Works
Wheelwrig
Bolt

GROUND FLOOR

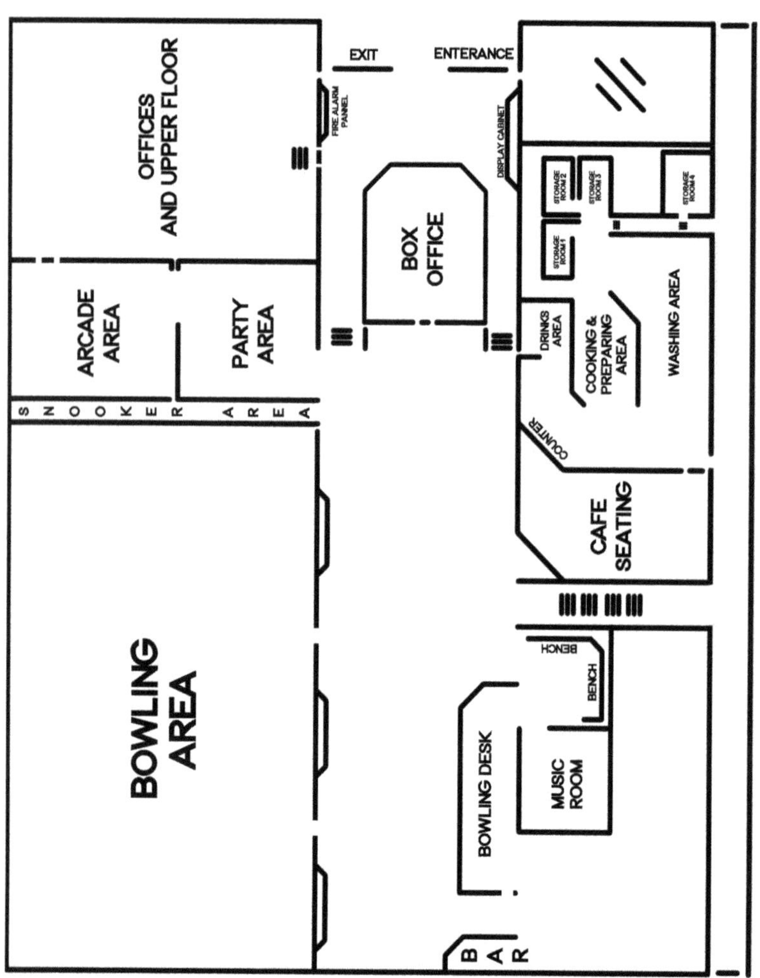

To obtain the best possible viewing angle of the plan of the ground floor map please, when required.. for a period of time of your discretion, tilt the book, by hand, to an angle so that the exit and entrance is on the right hand side of the page and the bar area of on the left with the book in a horizontal position.

Applying to all maps henceforth, but only detailed here, I ask that the Reader understands that the size of the map is the largest (of this I have done my best to ensure) possible size that print has allowed me to obtain in this 13 cm x 20 cm book. Please take things such as safe margins and alike into account as to why the maps, and those that follow, do not cover an entire page. Such is my confidence that I feel not it worth the attempt to spread the picture across two pages at the risk of perhaps, at the time of the print run, loosing some detail and having money wasted.

I have done my best to label all areas in a font size suitable for reading when printed but with the possibility of some labels being too small the following labels are the one I foresee being at risk: exit and entrance, the fire alarm panel (located on the inside of the building directly behind the exit), the display cabinet (located on the inside of the building directly behind the entrance) and store rooms 1, 2, 3 and 4 of the cafe (the small square rooms inside the cafe area).

Where three lines are used close together they are designed to represent stairs.

Major details have been left out, in the case of: the bowling alley, the cafe, the arcade and the party area due to the vast objects, at any given time, these locations had within them.

At the front of the building, beside the entrance, where there is an empty square with three diagonal lines and no label it is important that the Reader notes that this is not a room and did not exist.

To the right of the map (if the Reader is holding the book vertically) or at the bottom of the map (if the Reader is holding the book horizontally) the long empty long corridor that runs beside or underneath (vertically - horizontally) the building is in fact outside of the building and is designed to represent the alley way, thin but long in length, that ran beside the building and on the other side was the Holiday Inn car park. The alley way had a locked thick gate at either end. One lead onto Pershore Street and the other onto Upper Dean Street at the rear of the building. In all my time only have I seen, and used, the rear gate (that was an arse to lock at the best of times.. I never did get the hang of it). Use of the gate was limited and often not needed. Only on rare occasions was this ever opened.

In the interest of providing context to the map (a feature that will follow for all maps.. please do excuse the repartition) the ground floor was the second social hub of the building, the first being the floor, one above, that the ice rink was located on. The second in command simply because the ice rink and its popularity outranked, at all times, the bowling alley with ease. Perhaps the: cafe, arcade, pool tables and party area at one point in time were meant to aid in the visiting and time spent on the first floor away from the ice rink but in all my time only the pool area and arcade really got visited and even then the pool area, at the best of times, was vastly more populated than the arcade. Very few memories remain of spending time in the arcade other than in one long lost summer with Matt and Sashi and another when I won an unknown sum of money on the fruit machine (the only time, to memory, I ever did win on those blasted things).

The bowling alley was outranked by the ice rink simply because of the amount of faults it had from day to day, without fail, as you'll read latter on in the manuscript.

The cafe area was always popular, perhpas more so than the staff it had could cope with. The staff mainly included, varying on the date: Iqbal, Natalie, Sean and I. Other names past through the doors but non remaind as long as we did. I'm sure names that I'm unaware of before my time of working at the building in 2013 have been left out simply because I did not know them. Natalie was the manager, if you like, of the cafe and bar area but I hold no reserve in saying that Iqbal was but the sole operator of the cafe with Sean and I filling in when required, or willing (as often we viewed skating more important and said no on many occasion whereby it would impeed a weekend of skating with our friends.. such was the workplace that you could get away, without being fired, doing this.. perhaps we were too innocent to realise the impression we made upon doing so). I once also almost got in very serious trouble after I let two females have free meals (a plate of one burger and a portion of chips) and was caught by Colin, the then rink manager (the highest manager that resided in the building). I only escaped because Iqbal saved me somehow, I still don't know what he said but it was clear what I'd done to all as I stood there dumbfounded unable to answer any questions that was asked of me. My job was never at risk at any time, to my understanding, but it was a close call. Where the girls worth it if I had lost my job? No. I'll be as nice to leave it at that.

Disabled access was obtainable via ramp that ran from the side of the box office and down into the party area although I left this out of the map by choice.

The office and upper floor play host to events such as hiding Rory's clothes (much latter on in the manuscript) and any information may have written about, but have now forgot, about the so called staff room. It is important to note also, on the subject of the office and upper floor, that whenever I list a floor name: ground floor, basement, second floor and third floor this upper floor is not included amongst that list. This upper floor was unique in that it connected to no other floors and simply existed on it's own out of sight and I doubt any of the customers, unless told or had previously worked at The Leisurebox, knew about it's existence (see further detailed maps at the end of this chapter to get a more in depth look at what the office and upper floor looked like).

I should also include that between the bowling desk and the bar were four doors: the female toilets, the male toilets, the door that led to the corridor beside the bar and the cleaners cupboard. While the corridor is detailed in the further map of the bar that follows the end of this chapter the others are not included on any maps, at the time of writing. I have left these all out by choice. I recall not a single one of these rooms playing a significant or minor role in the manuscript and therefore their existence is redundant.

It should also be noted that the stairs between the bowling desk and the cafe area are the stairs that led the bowling alley up to second floor, the ice rink, as the ramp, outside, was only used, in 2012-2014, in emergencies. In 1965 and much after it was used as the only way up to the ice rink as the bottom floor was perhaps a separate venue and only during operating under The Lesiurebox did the building have stairs, at a high price of some multiple thousounds, installed. I recall Kevin or Lee telling me so (both managers). The design, in my ground floor map, of the stairs is not true to how they where but hard I have found it to attempt to put the scale of their true design onto a map and therefore what you have before you is my attempt. The stairs actually looped back on, and up, themselves a total of two times in order to reach the landing (a small square area that was decorated with perhaps a few pictures on the wall but nothing else.. the carpet was grey in colour and the location generally bland.. beside answering phonecalls no one spent much time in this space other than to make their way up or down the stairs) that resided outside of the double doors that led to the ice rink.

THE OFFICES

STAFF ROOM
UN-USED ROOM
CASH AREA
MANAGERS OFFICE
COLINS OFFICE
WORKSHOP
CORRIDOOR
CORRIDOOR
CORRIDOOR
BOWLING PIN SETTERS & MACHINERY

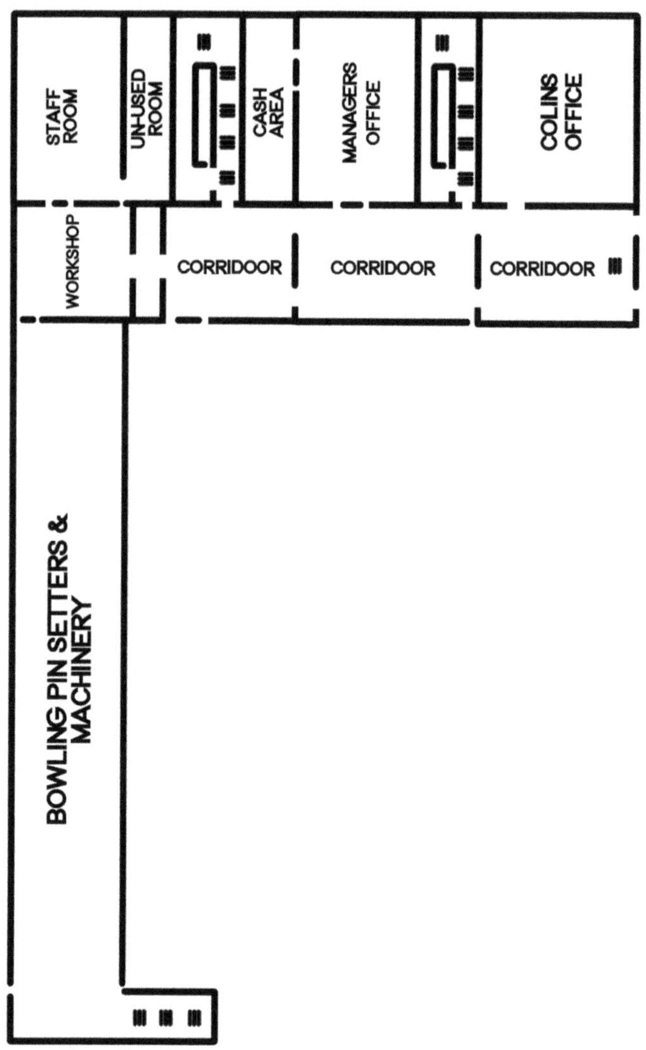

As, I believe, previously written I have made it clear that the upper floor, as I refer to it, forms no part of my naming of the floors. I consider it a side floor that served no purpose in the modern day although during during my countless visits to it signs did exist that once it was designed to serve a purpose.

All I will say regarding the upper floor, here at least, is that the stairs (again signed by three lines close together.. twice occurring on the picture to the left.. again best viewed horizontally) on the map to the left of this page, the two sets, are how one would get to this upper floor. Due to the distance of the second set of stairs from the main door we (I and whoever else visited this upper floor) never used them. A CCTV camera was present outside the managers office, as I recall, and therefore to go past the office towards the workshop was a no no for anyone that wasn't supposed to be by the workshop. You had to be invited into the workshop not just wonder in. I laugh looking back at how secret the managers liked the workshop to be. I only went in a handful of times as a result of this strange rule. Further information follows in the next chapter.

The corridor located next to, or underneath, Colins office (horizontally - vertically) was the first of three, and the small bit at the end, that formed an entire straight line of corridor's that spanned from the door that led to the box office all the way to the workshop.

As soon as you walked through the door you had a small landing area, useless, and then some steps going downwards. Colins office had a huge window that ran to the right hand side (walking down the steps away from the box office) and a singular enterence and exit door, no other way in or out. In front of his office doorway was the clock in machine attached to the wall on the left. You had two card holders and you punched the card into the machine and then put it on the other side to clock in and then vice versa when clocking out. A retro machine that still worked well (beside the times we took photographs of our cards to ensure we got paid correctly since we had to hand them in to get counted up in preparation for payday).

Through the first door and you would have the first set of stairs leading to the upper floor on the right and again a pointless empty area.

Through the second door and to your right would be the singular enterence into the managers office. As detailed on the map the cash area is where the safe's were located. I've no idea how they got the safe out the building when it closed and before now I've never much gave it a moments throught. I can only conclude it's either burried under the foundations of the now housing complex or got removed and destroyed (or sold on) when the workers were digging the building out of the ground bit by bit. I can only assume they built the building around the thing since there was no way that was put in afterwards.

Through the third door would be the second set of steps to your right, the ones no one dare use, and a door on the left that on the other side was the arcade area. Straight ahead was the door, most probably locked, that led into the workshop area.

On the inside to the right of the workshop was a small room that was only used by the guys that worked the pin setters and contained a few chairs and a radio, to my memory.. again I visited perhaps only a handful of times and therefore could be wrong. I also recall a room attached to it full of junk but could be wrong here also.

To the left of the workshop was a doorway that led to the back of the bowling machines, the dangerous area. Dangerous because, as you'll read, the roof leaked and therefore many machines had to be turned of when it rained so we didn't end up with a dead staff member post shift, and that's no joke. The puddles at the back of those lanes where a joke and beyond a hazard.

At the end of the long walkway was a doorway that led down some very old curvy stairs made entirely of metal, like something you'd find outside a set of flats in NYC. I sensed, the few times I went down them, that the stairs were an original feature.. and sure showed their age. I loved them.

THE UPPER FLOOR

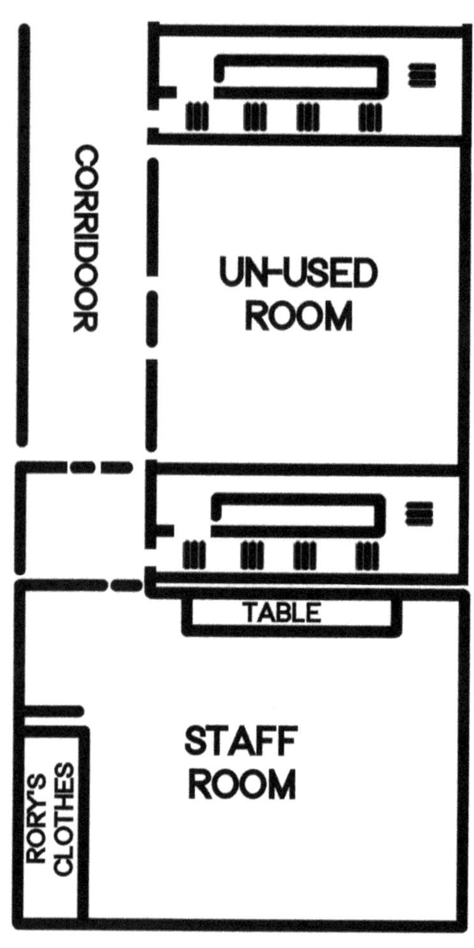

I promised more information but as you can see per the map I'm not sure what more I can give you.

The corridor has no end beyond the second set of stairs because I've long since forgotten what was at the end, if I ever went that far on my trip of discovery.

The un-used room is what I refer to when I write "probably had a purpose when built" or similar. This un-used room contained cabinets that could have been lockers and other things I've long since forgotten. Perhaps in 1965 or somewhere between it was designed to be the coat room while the staff room nearby was just that but with more things inside.

All that remained of the staff room today was a table, as per the map, and a couple of seats. The room had no ventilation and as a result of Kassum and Rory keeping their hockey kits up their all time it stunk. The main reason it never got used was because all the hive of activity was elsewhere in the building and therefore wherever you went, as a staff member, you had your own places that you liked putting things. On bowling it was the music room (a small room where the computer for the downstairs music was controlled). In the cafe it was a room out the back. In the bar it was anywhere since no one used it anyway and upstairs, skate hire, it was under the counter if not on the floor somewhere.

Colin tried to rally the troops, us staff, at some point between his being appointed as rink manager and closure of the building to tell us that he'd put a microwave and this and that in the staff room so we used it more but he never did and so it remained a dump. Colin did, however, put a dart board and TV's in the bar though, so fair play to him for that (the story of how the dart board became famous and almost got three people the sack follows in a latter chapter).

THE BASEMENT

There will be no map for the basement simply because of all the areas of the ice rink this is the one that I visited perhaps only twice during my stay. Once when I and Steph started work at The Leisurebox and once when we closed, as a final goodbye and so that the managers could give us a fright (of this I'm sure I wrote about also in a latter chapter).

What I can tell you is that whatever was down here had probably been since 1965. The only standout thing that I found cool about the basement was the big (and I mean huge) planet ice sign that was just sitting there un-used. I've no idea how it got down there since the stairway, as I understand it, was the only way up and down. The rooms, it had a few, contained anything and everything.. almost everything I forget. I remember one room was entirely flooded and we had to climb on the edge that ran around the inside wall to get a look inside so that we didn't drown in whatever gunk the water inside contained. The only light in that room was a torch.

The size of the pipes in the basement amazed me also. I don't think you'd believe me even if I did my upmost to describe them.

THE BAR

LANDING AREA
CORRIDOR
SEATING
SHELF
SHELF
POOL TABLE
THE BAR
THE BAR
LOCATION OF BARRELS & ALL PIPES
TABLE & CHAIRS
WASH AREA
UN-USED SPACE
BACKSTAGE AREA
STORAGE ROOM

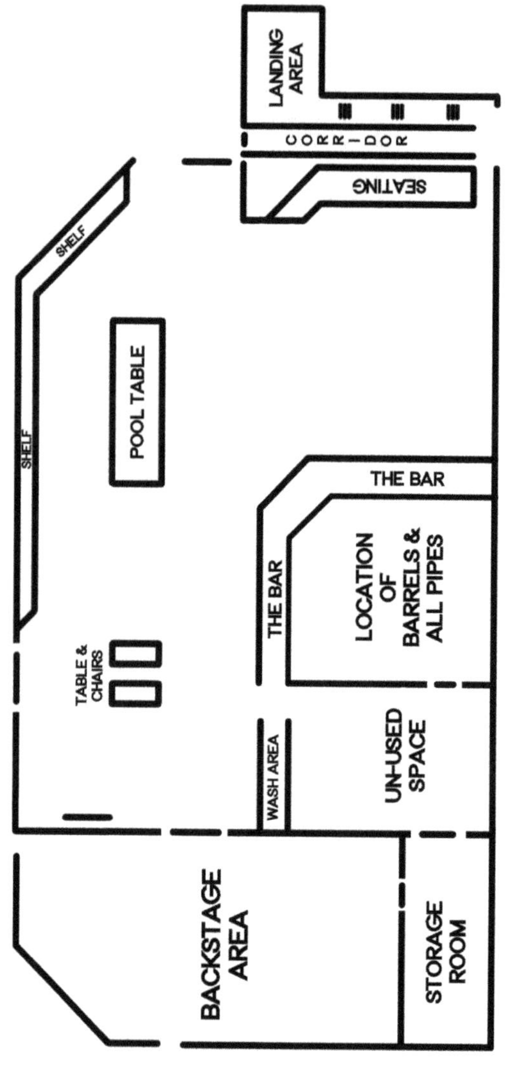

I feel maybe it's backwards to include the bar last but here we are (last of things on the first floor that is).

If you refer to the map on Page 9 you'll clearly see just how small the bar area is, an error I'm aware of in design. The map on Page 25, beside or above (vertical - horizontal) this one, provides a clear picture of what the bar area contained.

The bar features in *Part Two - The Story* often, including how I discovered it, and so, like all of them I suppose, worth referring back to.. if needed.

There's very little detail I'm able to share with you here that doesn't feature in *Part Two - The Story.*

What I could say, perhaps, is that the blank space between the seating area and the bar was closed off towards the end because of damage to the roof, we literally lost half of the room and the best place to fall asleep out of sight of everyone. That sofa really was comfy, if not a little hard to fall asleep on because it was so thin.

The door (highlighted on the map a single line in a gap of a wall.. if you've not yet realised) beside or above (vertical - horizontal) of the table and chairs is the doorway that led from the bowling lanes, the bottom few, into the bar. No one used them because they where so well hidden, a map couldn't do it justice.

The corridor was pointless and served only as a

a walkway from the main area downstairs in order to get out the back to the smoking area (the long thin walkway I described).

The stairs the lead up to the landing area is perhaps of most interest amongst the map of the bar for the stairs on the map was the only way in and out of this little area and the bar was the only way to get to it. I'm quietly confident that I detail this area in chapter in *Part Two - The Story* but in the interest of re-capping the basics it was a small area that was unlit and I never went up the stairs. An area, looking on from the bottom.. as I always did, you could mistake for a house. I've zero idea of the purpose of this area or what it was used for, in 1965 or 2014.

The wash area was but a sink and perhaps a mop. I never used it other than after one major event when we hosted a bowling competition or to, on the rare occasion, clean glasses out of the bar (so rare 99% of the glasses in the bar didn't ever get touched until Iqbal removed almost all of them when we shut.. with permission, of course).

THE ICE RINK

RAMP
RAMP
STREET LEVEL
RAMP
STORAGE ROOM 2
FIRST AID ROOM
WARM ROOM
FOOD ROOM
THIRD FLOOR STAIRS
EXIT
DJ BOOTH
STORAGE ROOM
FEMALE TOILETS
ICE RINK
CORRIDOOR
CORRIDOOR
COACH'S ROOM
ICE RINK
LANDING AREA
PENGUIN DESK
WENDY SKATE SHOP
SKATE HIRE
CORRIDOOR
OLD STAGE
ICE RINK
PD 2
HOCKEY ROOM
ICE PIT
MENS TOILETS
ICE RINK
FIRST AID
GARAGE
OLD ICE BAR

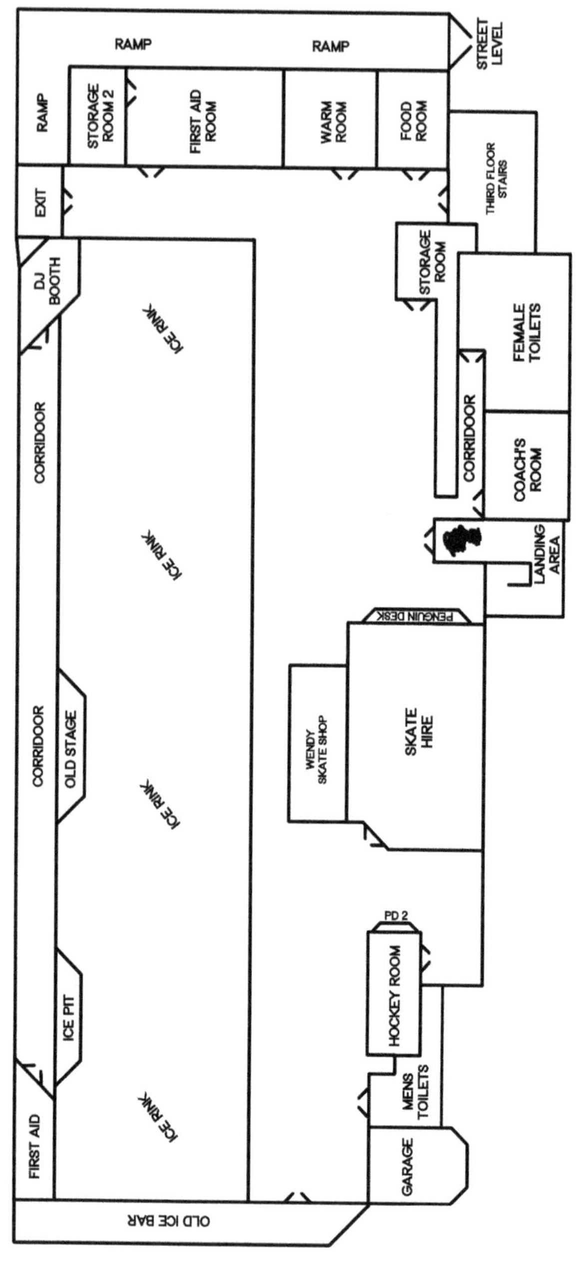

Any information I've not included about the first floor, basement or anything below the second floor in either the first part of the map section, every page from 5 - 28, or in *Part Two* or *Part Three* of the manuscript has either been forgotten or deemed pointless to include.

* *

Last to design but not last in the list. I've changed the doorway's to half triangles without a tip for this map simply because I've realised (as you do at the end) that it's easier than cutting out slits in the walls and filling them in with a door (as is on every other map beside this one).

I couldn't design the map last night but now look what I've created. I thinks perhaps the most detailed out of all the maps, and most refined at that. No doubt I'll re-create the maps at a latter date with either more detail, better scale or just because I'm always fiddling at so called finished projects although deem what I've created thus far to be accurate enough and any differences in either my design or elsewhere have been written up where and when required, I believe.

I hope this map is readable. I designed it in a 8000 x 8000 document instead of a 4000 x 4000 (pixels) like all the others because of the detail required. I might have to sell every issue of this manuscript with a magnifine glass at this rate.

Things that would be worth noting on this map is that the ice pit was actually not on the ice rink (as any sensible person would realise) but rather behind the wall that I've put it front of. It was a slit in the barrier than then droped the entire length of the building and had wooden doors that created a V shape if you stood over them and look at them from the ice pad. If you fell down there was no escape and while the doors should have been shut at all times they never were (I'm sure I detail this in more depth at a latter chapter).

The same then can be said for the old stage which in reality was the old DJ booth in 2012-2014 because the stage, whatever remained of it, had been destroyed. From old photographs (again you'll have to use Google because copyright) the stage looked, past tense, glorious but didn't really fit in with how the rink was in the more modern day. What remaind of the DJ booth, then, was nothing but a square box that had long since been abandoned and was far too un-safe to go inside. Again this old DJ booth was behind the wall that on the map it is in front of (so behind the wall out of sight not on the ice pad).

The first aid room (the one attached to the end of the corridor) is the old first aid room that contained some items but I never ventured inside. In the modern day, like everything behind the curtain and in that corridor, it was long since un-used.

The old ice bar contained matts, an un-used bar and other things that the room was too dark to see inside of (detailed in a latter chapter).

The garage was really where the Zamboni (probably not the correct name for our ice machine) was kept. Inside the garage was two Zamboni's (again.. shoot me) of which one was owned by Brian. I believe he let the machine go down with the building simply because it was worth nothing and couldn't get it out. In the garage there was a shutter that led out to a major drop on Upper Dean Street below it but they'd long since never been opened. You could see the drop and the shutters from Upper Dean Street if you Google view the location (73-75 Pershore Street, Birimingham UK). The garage also contained two other rooms: one had tools in and the other I am unsure. They where located directly at the back wall.

The hockey room had showers and a small un-vented room. People would use it to get changed for hockey but how non of them choked inside is beyond me because whenever I walked inside I went straight back out again. Towards the end the stewards used it as their private room but I sense they only did so to avoid paying for a locker (of which wasn't that much anyway). I don't feel sorry for them because rather you than me, mate.

Wendys skate shop was perhaps the most

interesting of all things that remained in 2012-2014 as it was adopted to be a skate shop when in 1965, and beyond that, it had been a way to get up to the third floor. Wendy's shop was really some skates thrown on the inside of the double doors and on the stone steps with a board behind them that from the viewpoint of the corridor or empty space beside the ice rink you couldn't tell that it was anything else but a small shop. I'm not sure she really got much business truth be told. I looked at the shop from the third floor the once and put two and two together, I sense the entire building was separated and ran by many different companies from 1965-2014 that I'm unable to trace due to lack of records or available historical resources.

PD 2 = Penguin Desk 2, the design is just too small to include the entire label. PD2 is where the desk was located towards the end. Penguin desk is where the desk was located when I talk about meeting Kerrie and Sashi or anything else referring to the same area (I'm sure there's quite a bit).

The first storage room I only went in once or twice and can't remember anything about.

The third floor stairs led both up to the third floor and down to the bottom that when the doors opened led out onto Pershore Street to the left of the entrance double doors (if you were standing looking face on at the building).

The food room was the storage room for all things that the vending machines needed.

The warm room was but a small room that contained the only heater on the second floor.

The first aid room was the one used in 2012-2014 and attached to it was another small room that had skates and other things in it (storage room 2). You could only get in this second storage room by going inside the first aid room.

The DJ booth, the one in use in 2012-2014 at the top of the map, could only be gotten into by going through the exit, next door to it.. a fire exit, and around the back. That then led onto the corridor as the DJ booth had a door inside of it. The DJ booth overlooked directly the ice rink and you could quite easily talk to the DJ while skating around.

The ice rink was perhaps more circular but for simplicity's sake I've made it square.

The ramp on the outside only features the downwards slope that lead onto Pershore Street but also went upwards towards the raised square platform that to dot on the map was between the first aid room and the warm room. On Google maps again you can quite easily see this raised platform section supported by long pillars that ran onto the street. In fact on Google maps you'll be able to see the ramp design quite clearly.

The landing area (with a little bit of a sketch) was what led down to the first floor with the bowling alley etc.

THE THIRD FLOOR

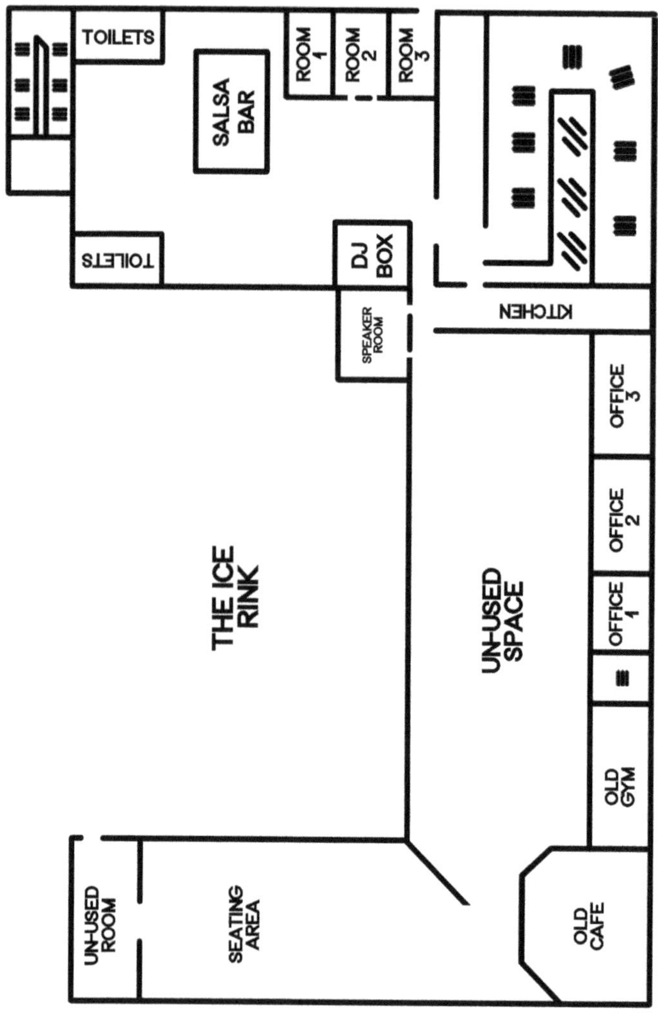

Any information I've not included about the second floor or anything below the third floor in either the second part of the map section, every page from 29 - 34, or in *Part Two* or *Part Three* of the manuscript has either been forgotten or deemed pointless to include.

* *

Loved it, could have spent my whole entire life at The Leisurebox on the third floor. I'm a wonderer (a non-existent word in the Englsih dictionary I fear) and often drift in and out of alertness regarding whatever it is I'm supposed to actually be doing, besides drifting around. The third floor was a person with a short attention spans wet dream. Endless amounts of history resided and mostly left un-touched from whenever it was last operational.

I should highlight that it is near impossible, with my ability, to get the depth required, in the map design, that the third floor alone deserves simply because of the vast array of things it contained. If there was a storage room in other companies we had a storage floor, and decades of it resides on that third floor.

A first note would be that where the ice rink is labelled the reader must understand that it is because when the building was designed (and of this fact, it is a fact, I am sure) in 1965 the third floor wasn't separate as it was in 2012-2014. Every edge (I consider there to be three edges for each wing of the upper floor) of the upper floor was designed, in 1965, to overlook the ice. I'm afraid Google will have to serve you these images as I don't own the copyright to any of them. In 2012-2014 all that remained of being able to see the ice rink from the third floor was the small cracks in the paint and the hole that remained in the room that is labelled speaker room. It's amazing how long you could spend inside there looking down at people skating past and they'd be totally unaware. Besides if you spent too much time in that room, the speaker room, you'd be deaf in no time at all and so not much time was spent inside.

In 1965, and for some time after, I believe the wing that the dance floor and salsa bar was on was seperate. There's a doorway that remained on the ramp that led to a set of stairs, boarded up I think, that ran up to the third floor. It had a badge above it. I assume it would have been left through the doors to the nightclub and back on yourself and up the ramp to the ice rink. I can be sure that the box office, in 1965 and for some time after, resided at the top of the ramp although had since been demolished.. the box that the box office staff sat in that is.

The part with a label of unused space could have been any number of things in the past. It had what remained of a cafe and a gym with changing rooms for males and females and offices. The largest of each wings in my opinion, based on memory.

The seating area had a plenty of fold down plastic seats and a little room at the end. I remember Andy showing I and Steph around for the first time when we started, I liked it up on the third floor from the moment I knew about it. The room was empty and overlooked the markets, I think.. we never went inside because it looked unsafe. All that resided inside was a bird that Andy had a name for, I forget, and lived in the hole in the roof on the hut. The windows that this room had were smashed and anything could fly in or out. Well, there was holes in the roof so that was possible regardless of this room.. I suppose. Thinking of it (and I fail to recall if I write this latter on) we spent a few days beating away birds that had flown in through the roof when open the public.. a hard one to explain that I'll admit.

For latter reference Rooms 1, 2 and 3 is where Siraj and I (and others whom I forget but latter include) play hide and seek (*Part Three - The Small Memories*).

The toilets were the weirdest bit. I went inside but the darkness put me of wanting to be inside for too long. Plus how exciting are toilets are the best of times? By the time I'd realised exploring the third floor was what I liked doing the building had closed. I took for granted it would always be here, out of sight.. my little secret.

The kitchen is the one that is perhaps designed poorly on that map. It was square but much longer than what I've made it out to be and contained machinery that had long since been left behind. It also contained a hundred and one (if not more) boxes of: socks, gloves, pencil cases etc and therefore was a little hard to walk around in. A sign of what was once a thriving business at the very least (the size of the kitchen that is).

The DJ Box was but a small raised platform that overlooked the entire nightclub and obviously where the DJ would have resided. No equipment was left there, sadly.

* *

Any information I've not included about the third floor in either the third part of the map section, every page from 35 - 39, or in *Part Two* or *Part Three* of the manuscript has either been forgotten or deemed pointless to include.

Part Two

The Story

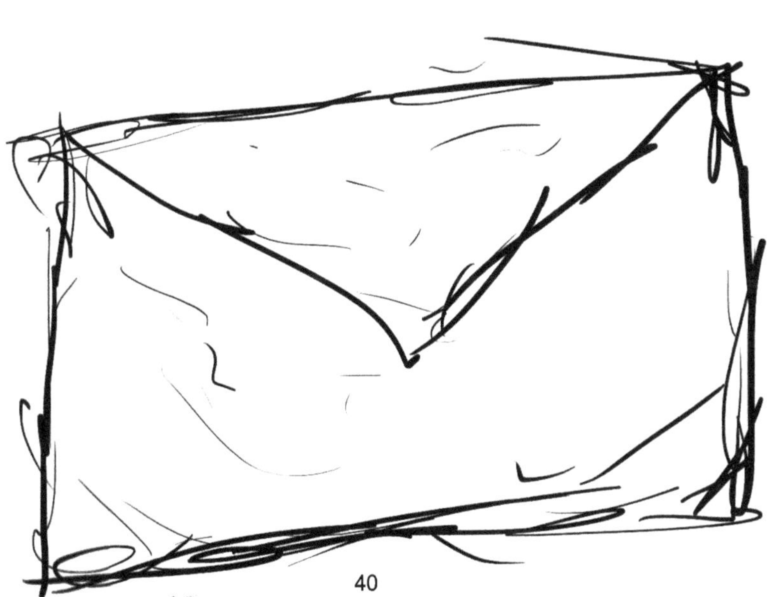

CHAPTER ONE

Sixteen years old is such a sweet tender age upon reflection. I feel old and wise now in comparison but I'm fully aware that being twenty one is tender also although more mature, I would hope. At sixteen years old it's common to think that you know all there is to know about the world and then suddenly the floor falls from under your feet and things change beyond recognition and everything your life has been about is over before you realize what's going on. Friends go, school ends and suddenly you're somewhat, beside your family, on your own to find a path in the world that you've no experience of. The world to sixteen year olds isn't a kind one, or at least wasn't when I left school as now things have changed so that you can stay on studying until you're eighteen. I'd decided long before school finished to join an apprenticeship in an area that then interested me, IT. College had never been for me. I'd gone from textiles with a room full of girls to a mechanics course at a local-ish college to graphic design, I ended up with a D post exams and a sour taste of the whole sorry episode in my mouth, so to speak. The college episode ended abruptly with a phone call I'd requested the office of the college to make to the school asking them to come and get me and let me go home because I'd had enough and then I assume they had gotten fed up at that point and took me of the course and found somewhere to put me, graphics of course. I think mostly the same characteristics I possessed then stay with me today and could have been a contributing factor towards not wanting to stay on. The course was run at a college that's roughly less than a handful of miles away from my house, today I could probably walk from home to the college location in 20-30 minutes, just to give you an idea of proximity before I continue. What annoyed me most was that while this course was run it was dark, and I assume winter, and therefore to get back to school, of which was the location they, the teachers, where adamant on dropping us of at, we had to go back past my house, or the road beside my house, to get to school. I asked once if I could be dropped off and they made an exception but beyond that they forced me to wave past my road and instead take me a further three to four miles in the opposite direction to schools location. Somehow, in their minds, asking me to walk all that way home again was safer for them than pulling over at the side of the road and allowing me to walk around the corner. I was sixteen years old and could make choices for myself thank you very much. I went toe to toe with them once I'd reached my limit and the phone call perused and so did the end of my college career. Besides the late night walking home annoyance the course overall was slow and rather classroom based, there's only so many hours in a day you can ask a dyslexic to stare at books and a whiteboard before they lose interest and get annoyed. I think I touched an engine a grand total of once and learnt nothing from that place, at all. There were no fit girls in the textiles group so I left that without blinking twice. Finally, well, the graphics episode ended because my time at school did. Truth be told I only really made it through because of Mr. Hassan and Mr. Jagidar (the head of technology and a graphics teacher retrospectively). To them both I owe a lot for their upmost of patience during my many attempts at causing a disturbance on an almost every lesson basis.

My school experiences above bears no real solid input towards the story here but merely plays a small part in my background leading up to it. I suppose the grandest contribution of all this episode was that it only confirmed that IT was the subject for me to take into latter life outside of school. A kid that first had a computer in the early 2000's and hasn't been alive in a time without them it's only natural things that I don't blink twice at some other people need educating on and if I could make a buck or two out of it, hey, why not, right? Being paid for learning felt like a more worthwhile path to pursue at sixteen and so it was settled, after an open day and maybe an interview, IT it was.

Months after leaving school, September time I think, while all my friends where enrolling on their first days of college and their adult lives I took a separate path and started mine on an IT Apprenticeship with a company called Zenos located on 127 Hagley Road, Floor 3. The summer between finishing school and starting adult life on the apprenticeship was a short one and the only thing I remember of it was catching up with a few old faces cycling all over the place and relaxing in the sunshine at all the local parks making the most of our short freedom in between protected childhood and adulthood that awaited us. GCSE results where ok but not brilliant, enough to get me onto the course but not really anything special overall. I've a knack of doing that mind, being able to scrape by when needs be. My proudest achievement was that I'd managed to achieve a Distinction, the highest possible grade, in IT.

On the first day and for the early part of the course everything was fine and dandy. The course that we had all enrolled on was advertised as a five or six month placement in classrooms and afterwards once you'd completed all that and gained your qualifications you'd go on to start your career outside the company in the proper industry and become minted for life. Well, maybe not minted (a slang word for rich I should explain) but you'd get somewhere, somewhere better than back to square one. As the weeks rolled on and the rose tinted glasses had been removed like taking candy from a child the course was obviously anything but what it had been advertised as. I suppose this is my one real chance in life, besides talking to those that were on the course with me, to inform the world what Zenos was really like on the inside. I don't really want to get too involved because in reality I escaped before it fell to pot too badly and got myself a job elsewhere. The facts are that the company fell flat on its face and after our year group no more studied at the company. Overall I've no idea why corruption and failings on every imaginable scale seem to spring to mind when thinking about the place. There was a lad on our course that had a heart problem and had to leave in the first few weeks and was promised a place on the next group the year after once we'd all finished, in truth and upon reflection it's him that I feel sorry for because I doubt he got to have a go at the career he'd wanted. None of us knew him well enough or know what happened to him after he walked out the classroom for the last time so there's no ending here, happy or otherwise, sorry.

I've skipped forward slightly in this so far tale of woe, it gets more positive I promise.

February 23rd 2012 was to prove a very special day indeed. Today, or this date rather, would be the date that we would say goodbye to Georgina Brooker and I would, for the first time ever, encounter The Leisurebox, although not for the last you'll be glad to read (although I can only guesstimate that the thickness of this book tells you that. Be a book for ants otherwise, right?).

By this point in the course we'd all established that something wasn't quite right but it was still early days on the scale of how long it would be until it all went to pot. I think we'd all gained our qualifications and where having no luck with chucking out CV's day after day on job websites, sure we got paid to send people our CV's but it was boring and with little progress, the same could be said about the internal job application process in the form of two career offices that were out of their depth. Uncontactable and making no real progress for anyone, I did get one interview at the local hospital but even then the course had sent several people for one position so that goes to show just how much they were struggling in that they had to give false hope to all but one of those several people to make, I assume, their figures look good. They didn't really make any secure connections with companies in the industry to take us on either at the time (I think eventually they made one and that's how they got rid of everyone that remained when they shut down but at the time it was another failing that would take a short while to rectify).

One person that did manage to escape earlier than most and make a shot in the industry was Georgina Brooker. As mentioned at this point she was leaving us and starting work at a local, to her, hospital. I think she got the job by herself hence why she managed to escape so early on the timeline. Good for her I say, one of the better ones that put the work in so was deserved.

Personally saying goodbye to Georgina was saddening because she was the person that I'd spent the past few months sitting next to at work every day. Sometimes we'd bring in sweets and sit and wolf them down as we job searched and others we'd sit and talk and giggle. Georgie was generally a person that made work more worthwhile. One memory I don't thank her for was pointing out and taking a picture of some white substance that I'd gotten on the top of my shoe one day and made a crude joke about, I never did live that down. As a person that was worth making an effort for it's no surprise that our class, our group, decided to do something different and somewhat exciting to make her leaving memorable. We'd discussed as a group that Bowlplex, located down the road, was boring and had been done to death, we wanted something new and exciting and so chose The Leisurebox. It offered bowling, again, but with the added addition of ice skating and it with this decision the rest that follows was set in stone. Even if Georgina was leaving inadvertently she left me with the biggest gift possible in the times that I had during the following two years of my life because of this chance encounter with the place. Au revoir Georgina, merci.

Like most days in my life I forget the parts that hold no significant value and therefore anything up to the point of walking into The Leisurebox for the first time is and shall forever remain forgotten. My earliest memory of the day in question is being steps away from the front of the building and approaching for the first time. Is it open? Where's the entrance? A topic that I'm sure confused many first time visitors, how to get in and if we were open that is. The place was like a Tardis (yes that's a doctor who reference) in terms of being bigger on the inside but appearing bland and nothing on the outside. The building did not hide its size but didn't appear anything special from the outside, worn and tatty if anything with a few posters here and there. The entrance was in fact hidden, somewhat, inside a small sheltered area. A sign reading The Leisurebox written in black bold typeface on a white LED background stood above, maybe in the middle, of the entrance and exit (of which were as plain jane as could possibly get in terms of design: two double doors either side). To my knowledge the lights never worked but where simply for visual effect, if anyone ever noticed them that is.

After we'd stumbled around the entrance for a while doing lord only knows what the doors finally swung open and had been done so by the security guard that stood inside the building on the doors. The guards name as it turns out was Rob and in the following two years would become a friend and someone of whom I'd attend one or two social events with. Also present was Pete the second and permanent, then, guard alongside Rob, over the two years he would also become a friend. Once inside we all huddled around standing by the small reception area making quite a bit of noise and not a whole lot of decisions. I've no idea and fail to recall what was so hard about paying the ten pounds or thereabouts for one game of Bowling and Ice Skating, unlimited might I add, but it took everyone beside I and Luke quite some time to achieve, a hard bunch us lot to organize at the best of times, considering there was no alcohol involved it might have taken longer than usual on this occasion. While I and Luke made our way down five or six steps and in to the closed cafe area on our immediate left to take a seat in the very hard and uncomfortable plastic chairs it was quite noticeable that the place, this being a weekday, wasn't exactly busy and was only really occupied by the staff, a regular occurrence I would latter find out.

After a short time, some fidgeting and a browse of the then Blackberry mobile that I owned the group finally joined us at the bottom of the steps. Turns out some had food in their bags and this wasn't allowed, not even to enter the building, pinky promise "I won't eat it honest sir" was no good here "Sorry, policy" and all that jazz. After another huddle and decision making we decided to try ice skating first, I'm sure the sun had set and risen many times during the time it took us to make this decision.

We made our way up some stairs, three sets in total, and finally arrived on the other side of another set of double doors and could finally see the ice rink, at long last. "It's cold" and "I'm holding onto the barrier" I'm sure was amongst many spoken first impressions. The confusing part, again, was trying to find skate hire. A task that latter, again, I would learn was not just us. After finding a sign on the wall with an arrow pointing towards the ice (and no thankfully we did not simply walk onto the ice like we did not possess a brain cell) we walked straight from end to end and finally found a small hut hidden around a corner that had a worker located inside. After exchanging our shoes for skates (rather you than me, mate!) we strapped them up and made our way onto the ice.

Unknown to me at the time rental skates where not the most pleasant of things and were latter known as the plastic fantastics because they where nothing but a hard plastic outer shell moulded with a blade fitted on a holder at the bottom and some thermal padding on the inside for comfort. Cheap one piece ice skates with blades sharpened by staff to reduce costs, rather than at a proper place, often meant uneven and rubbish cuts. Latter on in time I would become qualified, after attending a course at Coventry Ice Rink, to sharpen rental ice skates and as it turns out it wasn't a pleasant job at all. The most joyous part was being able to put the headphones in and block out the world while I did the same thing over and over again until I'd done enough pairs to satisfy the manager before I gave up and got bored and wanted to stop. The mask they gave me wasn't up to the job and the question of the damage that the dust that you'd no doubt inhale often came to question, "get on with it" we were told but is often why anyone but I, Big J or Connal did not touch the machine, JB and Steph where also trained and qualified but never did any as far as I recall. The only customer that did like my cut was Carl, a family man that would attend and text me every Friday to ask me to cut pair 120_. I think that's accurate, somewhat. The number system worked like 203 for pair #3 of size 2's and 701 for pair number #1 of size sevens. Basically it was 10_, 20_, 30_ and so on with the last number representing what pair of that size you had, all in all it was just a number that matched one written on the boxes inside skate hire and was a job of finding and matching them to give the person the correct shoes back. I did cuts for other customers from time to time as it wasn't uncommon to have skates of a size with no sharp blades at all but didn't really like to make a habit of it beside maybe on the weekends, cool kids seem to like sharp blades so they could show of in their fantastics to attempt to get a girls attention. Sure, I'll help you as best I can.

Once on the ice it somehow, to me, came naturally. No need for the barrier and no need to fall over just skate forward and enjoy. People said I was showing of and had done it before but I and the ice just jelled from the off. Luke was the only other person who had skated before but failed to mention it before this visit and we all found out as he was running rings around us while we all gently made our way around the ice. I seem to recall maybe one or two others being able to skate, somewhat, without the need of the barrier all the way around but the rest used one entrance point to another on the rink and then went back again and didn't really go any further. Poor Sona fell over at some point during the session and that was the end of that for her, no ambulance needed on this occasion, thankfully. I could skate in a straight line but couldn't corner and managed after a few laps by shifting my body weight on my feet to aid in my giant turning circle to get around the corner, no crossovers or hockey turns at this point thank you very much.

The skating didn't last long because beside I and Luke everyone else seemed to think that a brief encounter was more than enough time to render their purchase adequate. We'd both paid for skating and bowling and didn't really fancy bowling on our own without the group so we were forced to trade in the fantastics for our shoes and bolt, somewhat, downstairs to re-join the group who were by this point already getting their shoes and writing their names on a piece of paper for the employee to enter onto the system to start the game. A brief encounter that sparked two years of passion. Once was enough to know that this wouldn't be the last time I'd meet with this building or in particular the ice.

The bowling shoes I received, once I'd found the correct size, where, in my opinion, equally as tatty and as bad in physical condition as the ice skates where. Much later on, as a staff member, I'd find out that the only cleaning the shoes got was a quick spray with something contained within a bottle after every use (common it was to have to put your hand in front of the shoe around the back like a cup to prevent the cloud that the spray produced from making the customer choke and fall onto the floor). Unpleasant to say the least but unpleasant even more so when it came to me being the one cleaning the things fresh of the sweaty foot of some unknown person, much latter on of course.

With the bowling shoes, at last, on and a peg on my nose the game was all set up and ready to go. We had two lanes together. Two benches seated all of us and the bowling ball machine in the middle was the only division between us. The luxury prize was the spinning seat that resided in line with the bowling ball machine and in-between the benches. If you snooze you lost your seat and someone else would claim the throne and send themselves into a dizzy spell on the spinny seat.

As we had quite a large group it meant lengthy waiting times between each other's throws and when combined with how often and how many times the machine broke down it only delayed our game to a period of time that no doubt would have sent anyone doolally. I and the group wasn't alone in suffering at the hands of the awfully unreliable machines as another thing I would find latter on was just how many refunds had to be given due to customers complaining about the standard of the machines. The conditions that the lads out the back had to work in were quite dangerous and really looking back I'd say they where under paid for it also. It was a job you did out of love rather than because it made you any better off financially. It was dangerous as in that when it rained, heavy or not, the roof directly above the bowling machines, behind the boards and out of sight of the public, would leak and therefore the rain would fall down onto the pin setters and back of the machines meaning they had to be turned off to prevent electrocution and possibly fire. Quite common to walk the alley at the back of all the machines and find you would have to jump over or endure big puddles of water on the floor. Thankfully that wasn't my work place and a job that was designated to the select few so not a site I saw that often but does explain, somewhat, the condition of the machines and the reason they broke down so often. You couldn't do anything as a staff member really beside say sorry and move them and offer them a free game on the house. Once I'd worked there long enough I understood that I didn't need to call up a manager to ask if the customer could have a free game or not because it was just the done thing. I'd do it because it's how we, whoever was unlucky enough to work on bowling during any given shift, kept the customers happy in the end. Sure the company lost money but it got us through our shifts, if even only for another day.

Once we'd finished our game of bowling, eventually, I and Luke both wanted to make our way back upstairs to continue ice skating but it was clear that the length of the bowling game had taken it out of the others and that was enough for one day. It was more of a social trip and short hop than I had planned in my head and therefore was disappointed at how cut short it was. Again it wouldn't be the last time that I'd encounter the building, ice and everything else inside, but it certainty felt like I wasn't ready to leave my new surroundings just yet.

Removing the peg from my nose and putting my own, at last, shoes on we all then made our way towards the exit. Once outside I recall we all walked towards the Bullring and said our goodbyes to one another and to Georgina and then off we all went in our separate directions. A quick bus trip latter and normality had settled back in. Well, as normal as life would be from this point onwards.

CHAPTER TWO

Normality resumed and Georgina was of into the sunset on a brand new adventure meanwhile most of us returned to the same old dull office with the same old familiar faces. I, however, was minus a plus one and beside me resided an empty space that once Georgina had filled. There would be no one to fill it since the aim of Zenos was to get rid of us as soon as possible after our exams rather than to recruit more so I had no choice but to get used to it. It all kind of went downhill from here, work wise that is.

The job was a Monday – Friday, 9am – 5pm and paid the hourly rate of a grand sum of £2.65 per hour. After the week was done, as you'd expect, I was quite deflated. Friday evening would be spent travelling home in the rush hour traffic and eventually once I returned home the only thing that would become doable was to unwind and sleep. Amongst the inability to do anything on a Friday night lay the inner joy that the weekend, at long last, was almost here.

I and Luke came to the agreement (after many discussions during work hours that really could have waited but instead didn't and thus we both got, somewhat, a talking to by our group instructor to get back to something work related until we'd end them and then we'd carry on some more) that Saturday would be our day to ice skate. We both agreed that the brief encounter with The Leisurebox was far too short and that there was more to come. For Luke whom had, as said previously, skated before it was reigniting a passion long forgotten and for me it was a whole new world to enter into. At sixteen years old the enthusiasm for such an unknown to me activity was beyond words. A sheltered life up until this age it would be this point whereby everything I am today and quite a bit more was learnt and moulded. If the decision to visit The Leisurebox for the first time was sealing my fate then this decision with Luke was adding duct tape around the edges of the box that contained my fate to ensure nothing would get in the way to prevent it from playing out as it should.

A typical Saturday in this era would start between approx. 11am-12am and then end approx. 4pm-5pm. I and Luke would meet just yards from the location we said goodbye to Georgina, The Bullring, and make our way down towards The Leisurebox of which was located at most a quick five minute walk away, five minutes for our then young and energetic legs anyway.

Once on location, The Leisurebox, Rob, as usual, would swing the doors open just as he had the first time and many more to follow to welcome us in. I'm sure he recognised us as having visited before at this point but by no means where we on friendly terms, I think it was just something they had to do to welcome people and get them in. Manners cost nothing and all that. I think at this point in time, approx. 2012, the security guards and company as a whole was in its most serious faze that I witnessed during my entire stay. In 2012 things where serious and the business was run as a business but as things progressed it become more relaxed and of course by the end of it all had gone downhill completely and the building closed. I should clarify that going downhill means things where not as good in 2014 as they were in 2012 and nowhere near as many customers came through the doors, even on the weekends. Relaxed in that despite the disagreement of the managers you had security guards that would sit in the cafe come closing time and do nothing, not on the doors, not telling people to move on, just sitting and being lazy. Not Rob nor Pete because Pete had moved on and Rob was elsewhere with work at this point. There's no need for names but things had changed for sure towards the end.

Once we'd had our bags searched and paid I and Luke would sprint upstairs towards the second floor that the ice rink was located on. I always remember that halfway between the 1st and 2nd floor where the big white canvas pinned up on the wall was located is where you would start to feel the thud of the music on the floor and begin to hear it. The ice rink had an unknown to me number of speakers that weren't really the best they could be but did the job. Probably more in their prime in 2012 than 2014. They were meant to get replaced at some point for a new and better sound system but it never happened. The Leisurebox was a place of make do and mend not put money back into it. I think for some years everyone that ran a business inside the building has operated the same way and ultimately it was this mentality that closed the place down because there's only so many years a shell of a building can go uncared for before it becomes unsafe. I don't believe it was unsafe. I believe the owner wanted the land sold and his money because greedy guts. Letting Kevin and Iqbal, before my time, walk on the roof to fix it was unsafe in comparison. Music in this era that the then DJ played was far better than what came much later on. Not because the DJ then was any better than the two latter DJ's we had but because the music on the whole was more enjoyable. More people, better music, genuine enjoyment, it was the prime era. I still have many songs on my phone and windows media player and think of the ice rink when they come on. Soppy but I'll admit that when some come on I have to turn them off because it kind of reminds me that The Leisurebox did exist and everything was once real, it all feels so long ago you start to forget and question if any of it really happened. Music for me brings it all back and sometimes it's just too much of a loss to remember.

Once we'd bolted up the last set of stairs and through the double doors and finally worked our way through the sea of people towards skate hire we'd, again, exchange our shoes for skates and once more be reunited with the plastic fantastics. Providing we were both lucky enough to get a pair that all three fasteners on either boot did up properly and where not broken we'd then put our stuff away inside a locker and make, as quickly as possible, our way towards the ice ready for our four to five hours of pure enjoyment. The moment the blade impacted and made a groove in the ice for the first time was a sign that the weekend was truly here. We'd get on the ice together and then loose each other in the sea of people skating round until we'd eventually bump into each other for a quick chat only to then and almost instantly be taken apart from one another again. At this point the ice rink was only at half capacity because of the state of the ice on the other side due to damage caused in Christmas 2010, I believe. The amount of people that visited on a Saturday was unreal and moving was near impossible. It was quite common to spend half you session bumping into the person in front, beside or behind you because we were packed like sardines in a tin. I think the ice rink had a capacity of 400 at full size but it felt like they let that many in with only half a rink, if not more.

My skill certainty had not improved, at this point, since we had first skated and therefore was still attempting to make my way around the corner in the same way that I had on our first visit, by shifting my body weight on the feet. Problem that I quickly realised was that when you don't have the entire ice to yourself to take as wide a turning circle as you need it suddenly becomes very difficult. If anything it was really quite obvious quite quickly that if this was something that we were going to continue with then we'd both need to improve and brush up on our skills quite quickly. Added insult to injury was the fact that in this era the popular group, if you like, would stand in a circle by the DJ booth / first aid room and perform all their tricks, talk to one another etc to their hearts content. I think the unwritten rule book stated that I nor anyone outside of the popular group shouldn't bother any of them or enter their space and they won't cause you any trouble. It's laughable writing this and thinking about it but it was serious back then, to me at the very least. I'd compare it to the scene in Soul Boy, the film, when Joe challenges his fellow soul enthusiast to a dance off for prime space front of stage, it meant something to be amongst the popular lot, a symbol.

Back then I could skate around for far longer than I can know because the atmosphere and my energy levels where far more than what they are today. Even so I had my limits and once in a while I and Luke would reunite and decide to take a short rest stop and sit at one of the many tables that reside next to the ice rink barrier. It was a bit of a con that you couldn't bring your own food and drink in because just like every vending machine in existence the drinks are overpriced as is, more so, the food, if you can call it food. Nevertheless we were forced into buying something and would refuel our energy levels while watching the party continue, temporarily, without us. Once in a while we'd venture into the warm room because the temperature inside the rink was very cold indeed but mostly avoided because it was filled with the popular kids and even when it wasn't it was hard to get a space. I remember Richard the Jamaican cleaner used to come in with his hoover and clean the place up. I'd forgot about Richard because he was gone before I even became a steward, one too many arguments with kids outside the ice rink I think, I never did think to ask. Seemed a nice bloke anyhow.

Once we'd finished our snack and probably drank half if not more of our drinks we'd put them back in the locker and make our way, once more, onto the ice. I'd guesstimate that we maybe stopped once or twice during the session and beyond that we did nothing but skate. I'm too old to do it like that now and spend more time standing around talking than skating but back at this point we were full on. Something about the place always left me with a feeling of never wanting to leave, I'd always want to stay as late as I could. When I left I felt like I was missing out on something and that somehow it wouldn't be there to return to. Of course for a couple of years it always was but the feeling stayed with me to the very end and eventually would be my downfall in forgetting it because the one time I did the place closed down, typical.

When the clock reached anywhere between 4 pm - 5 pm it was time to go. The ice rink was open latter than that, way latter, but I think Luke was the limiting factor in how long we stayed and whenever he went I'd go as well because I knew literally no one and skating on my own didn't seem appealing at all. I was a bit clingy but having had a sheltered existence up until then it's somewhat self-explanatory. In brief my ability to feel comfortable in an environment without someone I know or to talk to was non-existent. I'm not assigning blame to Luke for making us leave but he always made out he had a long way to get home and therefore like to leave before it got dark. In reality Northfield is not that far away and was one bus down the Bristol Road home but I knew no different back then. I don't think he much like the travelling and as time wore on it would become his downfall and eventual withdrawal from skating all together.

Empty locker, get shoes back, say goodbye to Rob and heading home we were. I've no idea at what point we parted ways but our bus stops where on two different sides of town so the walk together was brief. We'd always see each other two days later at work so it wasn't a big deal.

After another quick bus ride home I would arrive back at base much more deflated and hungry than when I left. Until another week that was it. A week was always far too long to wait but it made it that bit more special. We left before lights out and the party always shined from the moment we got there to leaving so we never did see the before or after and instead enjoyed only the prime time.

CHAPTER THREE

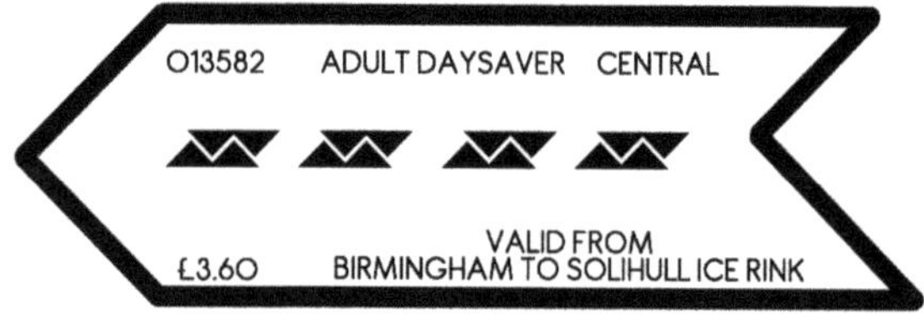

I and Luke settled into a routine and approximately three months down the line we were still enjoying it just as much if not more than ever. I'd never really had a hobby before this because it had basically been school and then straight, at least it felt like it, into Zenos and then I discovered The Leisurebox before the Zenos episode was even over so it's hard, in a way, to remember a time in my life whereby The Leisurebox didn't exist. I'd guess that's why if you combine the aforementioned reason with the fact that I was just only sixteen years old upon first visiting then it's probably why for me the building and every moment I lived between then and to the end holds so fond in the memory.

Three months was a long time and by this point both I and Luke had agreed that it was our time to get some of our very own ice skates. The plastic fantastics had been great and all but we were ready to progress, or at least felt so. Our limiting factor was budget as getting paid £2.60 per hour approx. left us with only a weekly income of £91 - £93 pounds per week and ice skates, depending on what brand or pair you wanted, could quickly become a whole lot more expensive than that. The basic pair that appealed to us where Bauer Vapour TI's that cost a grand sum of £65, an expensive luxury to a sixteen year old who's only purchase of value that I recall at that point was my very first mobile in the form of a Blackberry.

With the £65 saved the day finally arrived to make the long awaited purchase. We'd both spent many hours during work doing our research and looking at different pairs and getting told of so we decided it was about time to make the purchase before we got into any real trouble for being on websites that we shouldn't be during work hours. I make our tutor at Zenos, Qasim, sound like a grumpy bloke but in reality he was a fresh faced lad with a sense of humour and some good knowledge behind him, I'd spare an afternoon for a catch up.

I took the bus into town and walked a short distance from my stop to Birmingham Metropolitan College where Luke was waiting outside and after a quick hello and chat we made our way to the even closer bus stop of which was only a few meters away. Being a sheltered clingy sixteen year old I hadn't done much travelling and as Luke was the older one I trusted him to get me there and back in one piece. I wish I'd known then what I know now because the whole thing could have been over and done with within a couple of hours instead of him taking me on the grand tour of Birmingham. The bus we got on was the No. 72 when in reality all I needed to do was walk 10-15 minutes down the road and get on the No. 60 or No. 957 and could have been there in about half an hour plus the time it takes to walk from the Coventry Road to the ice rink. I should add that we were visiting Solihull Blue Ice, as it was known then but is now Silverblades Solihull, because The Leisurebox did not have a skate shop. Well, not like Solihull did. Wendy, I would latter learn, had a skate shop that sold second hand figure and hockey skates but as far as I recall from my time working there she never really did shift many pairs and I'd say mainly because not many people knew about its existence as it was open by appointment only and figure skaters had weird hours and so didn't really suit many customers, bit of advertising wouldn't have gone a miss. Another viewpoint is that I and Luke knew no one at this point so you can't find out information from someone you don't talk to.

If you're interested I'm sure National West Midlands has the No. 72 bus route planned out with all the stops on their website or available somewhere on Google or alike but in the interest of saving you from enduring the same tedious trip that we had to, as I've already said, it took us on the grand tour of Birmingham beyond any distance I'd been used to before. All I remember about getting there was mile upon mile, some shops and plenty of awkward looks to and fro with Luke like "and we there yet?" and then glancing, once more, out the window.

Once stopped, eventually, the good thing was that the No. 72, of which was probably helpful to I and Luke at that point, was that it stopped right outside the building the ice rink was located in. Well, somewhat. When we arrived at location on Hobs Moat Road we could see Solihull Blue Ice written in big letters on the front of a building but all that was underneath it was a range of businesses from a snooker hall on the very end to a couple of restaurants on the other. We had a poke around and couldn't find anything. The businesses are more night time operated around that area and so at this time of day everything was empty and I don't recall many people being around, if any. After walking up and down looking at the same windows, doors, signs etc that we had for a while we finally found, beside the snooker hall, an alley way that lead down to a set of double doors. The penny dropped and we realised we'd finally found the ice rink. I'm not sure if we both were dopey but it wasn't really well advertised with signs or alike as to its direction for new customers. The next snag in the plan was that the doors we walked towards, and maybe into, where actually the exit and the entrance was located around the corner. Once, finally, inside we announced what we were there for and where allowed through the barrier, through a set of double doors to then turn back on ourselves and through a singular door into their reception area and skate shop.

On the wall and as pictured on their, at the time, website their skate shop was nothing more than a few skates hung on a wooden wall with price tags underneath. The Bauer Vapour TI's as promised where sitting on their own plastic ledge with a £65 underneath. We hadn't phoned ahead so where lucky upon reflection that there and then they had those skates in our sizes. I think the idea of one of us getting skates and the other having to come back and collect at a later date or wear the plastic fantastics for another session wouldn't have gone down well at all.

We had no idea how ice skate sizing worked or even that it had its own system compared to regular shoes as Birmingham only asked for your shoe size and gave you skates based on that and so with the help of the assistant we tried on our desired skates until we got the correct sizes respectively. Luke went first and was done with quickly in comparison to myself. In a shoe I'm about an 11-12. Mostly 11 but I like to say 12 because you know what they say about big feet, bloomin bill for new socks cost an arm and a leg I tell the. I always remember this part because Luke wouldn't let me live it down. "Take your shoes off," simple enough, only for the assistant to then discover my thick white England socks and Luke was all like "Why on earth did you wear them things? You didn't think this through." None of us had in truth, two pairs of thick socks is the way to go if you go ice skating with a third fresh pair kept in your bag to wear after you've finished as your feet will no doubt sweat. Don't ask why two pairs, it's the rule, as someone who's worked at an ice rink and skated for years just take the advice and act upon it, thank me latter.

Another snag in the day's events was that while I say I'm a size 11-12 in a shoe it turns out that in Bauer Vapour TI's I was a 8 ½. I've no idea how it works but such is how the day went down and the rest is history. £65 handed over, ice skates into big brown boxes and out the correct exit door we went back towards the bus stop located near enough at the end of the same alley way we'd walked down to get in ready for the grand No. 72 tour again. I think the grand treasure in life would be to find the receipt from that day and have it pinned on my wall but it would be another two years plus before the significance of that purchase sparked any light bulb in my head so it's no surprise it's probably long gone. I don't think I've even got the Bauer box anymore.

When the bus arrived, at long last, we boarded and sat next to each other on separate sides of the bus in the seats closest to the middle of the bus. I believe we had people either side of us and the bus was very busy indeed and therefore this was our best solution. Cramped and uncomfortable but better than standing.

After the grand tour was over we got off the bus somewhere in Birmingham and the rest of the day is somewhat a blur.

I have photographs, still to this day, that we took in the bus shelter outside Solihull Blue Ice while waiting for the No. 72. I and Luke where both so excited about our purchase that we uploaded photographs, after taking them, of our ice skates onto social media to share with the world of the next big step in our adventure. I don't recall if anyone played an ounce of attention.

As it turns out despite my initial findings ice

skate blades as they come from the factory are not very sharp. Initially I did test, regrettably, with my finger by rubbing it against the blade with my finger at angle and, to no surprise, it hurt but later on, much latter, I would learn that the blades could become quite flat and useless after just one session. Clearly my experience was still lacking. Laces are considerably better than straps and buckles and allow a much tighter, more personal, fit to the foot and therefore a more secure boot that provides more feedback and a better feel for the ice. Annoying to bed in at first and required tightening quite often but did the job a lot better than the fantastics ever did. The fantastics had been great at keeping us safe during our baby steps but they'd run their course long ago, thankfully.

The most two significant things those skates did do was (1) I would learn to stop in them (2) I would talk to someone other than Luke while wearing them for the first time. Both interlock with each other. A female's voice sounded, talking to me, during a session saying "drag your foot behind you like this." A female whom was softly spoken, small in height, red hair and easy on the eye. I took her words of wisdom and acted upon them and soon learnt how to drag the foot to come to a stop. I fail to recall the name of it but I much prefer a hockey stop or the one where you put your foot out in front of you at an angle to cut into the ice and slow down gradually. I use the latter of the two aforementioned stops most often however can only use my right foot on the latter of the two whereas some people can do both left and right individually or both at the same time

The females name, it turns out, was Sashi and we would, over time, become good friends up until approx. 26th-28th of May 2013. She stopped skating at the aforementioned date due to health issues and we haven't seen each other since (full closure is provided in chapter ten).

CHAPTER FOUR

Time advanced and I and Luke continued to skate on with the same old routine of once a week, every Saturday, for quite some time with the same maintained enthusiasm as the first time we visited. Saturday after Saturday, week after week, hour after hour. We managed it, for a while, but then as exciting as it was: the atmosphere, each other's company, the music, there was defiantly an inner feeling that more people in our social group was needed. It wasn't that I or Luke wasn't enough for one another but that a third person, or more, would not go unappreciated in our attendance. There would be one person, once, that would come to our rescue. Enter Michael.

Michael a.k.a The Kraken was older than I or Luke and attended the same course as us at Zenos and studied in the same class. Michael was our third amigo while at work and for this session would extend our friendship to a new experience. Michael was one of the people that was unable to attend The Leisurebox the first time we visited to say goodbye to Georgina all that time ago hence why it was a new experience. Well, for him at least. We all got on so well at Zenos that for ages I and Luke asked, asked and then asked some more for him to visit The Leisurebox even just once but for a long time he refused. Eventually Michael caved in, thankfully. It took much convincing.

As the story goes once upon a time on an ordinary Saturday long ago in a forgotten part of history Michael finally caved in and joined us. My limited memory forgets most of the detail and it starts with us three: I, Luke and Michael already at the ice rink with skates on mid-session. As stated above Michael had not skated before and so I and Luke had underestimated what this meant. For me it had come naturally and for Luke his learning was somewhat long ago done, the basics anyhow. Michael however had yet to grasp the basic concept of balance and Bambi on ice would be a generous comparison, for Bambi. I mean not to insult Michael. The balance issue was easily solved much in the same way that the group had done all that time ago in entering on one part of the ice rink and skating besides the barrier to the next exit and so on and so forth until getting bored, something many new comers found natural apparently. On one occasion it was the case that Michael had become somewhat adventurous, or lost, and made his way beyond the exit he normally took and round the top of the ice rink to the DJ booth, or the area closest to. The significance of this location was that because at this point the ice rink was at half size, still, it meant that the hard barrier met the soft blue matts and therefore holding onto them while skating was somewhat a lot harder if not near impossible. Forced with option of braving the new world or returning to familiar ground Michael performed a 3.0 U-Turn and attempt to make way against many bodies in the wrong direction towards the exit. An option that on our group visit would not have caused the slight bit of fuss given it was empty but on a Saturday it was near suicide. Not only had he entered the area of the unknown popular group but had decided to cause chaos amongst it. I don't think it was populated at that point, thankfully. I also over egg, somewhat, the position the kids that could skate held on the place. Dramatic effect for writing and all. He survived, thankfully, and eventually made it to dry land. I don't recall him making this attempt to adventure to the new land any time during this session further. Another story from this encounter, again about Michael, how can it not be, would be another further moment of madness, or again getting lost, and ending up, somewhat, in the middle of the ice rink. It took two full size stewards to pick him up and bring him back to the barrier after many slips and slides. I fail to recall, sadly for humours sake, if Michael fell over or not but it was a sight that had to be seen to be believed when a man of Michael's stature had to be carried underarm by another man to make it back to dry land. I don't think I'd of dared mention this, humorous or not, back at the office. The idea of getting size thirteen's up me rear is not a joyous one. Disclaimer: size of shoe may also be over written for dramatic purpose.

Hours later and after I and Luke had had our fun skating past Michael time and time again laughing at how he was unable to join us we'd all had our fun, well two of us at least, and decide it was time to call it a day. Everything was routine until we approached the double doors at the top of the stairs ready to leave and suddenly a voice called from a table nearby and was attempting to gain the attention of Luke. The female's name, unknown at the time of course, was Kerrie and after a short conversation they swapped numbers and we continued, all three of us, on our way. Michael, to my memory, then responded with similar to "go on Luke, you've pulled" meanwhile Luke grins taking it in his stride. It was true, somewhat, that he had pulled but history would tell us, and I'll tell you now rather than latter, than in the long run this moment of passion between two OK looking youngsters was not to last beyond physical attraction. Sorry dear reader. This is a memoir rather than fiction after all. *Besides Kerrie this would, somewhat, be our first encounter with Sashi. No conversation was had nor did she acknowledge any of us and instead sat quietly looking rather dull, tired and bored staring at her blackberry as the minutes during her visit passed by.

Back at the office Michael had something to counter Luke's story about him falling over and one that Luke could not deny in the constant grin on his face. On the other side of the coin was the fact that at least one of us, Luke, had escaped each other's company and managed to get acknowledged by someone on the outside of our social circle within the ice rink. Call it, somewhat, an advancement on our two man band but really was Luke and Kerrie rather than all three of us. I recall many an awkward session sitting on the sidelines while they chatted with nothing but vending machines and disco lights to pass the time. I really do wish, looking back, Michael would have stood up straight for something just past two seconds so that he might, just might, have entertained the idea of returning even once more. Sadly history tells us that Michael never returned again and beyond that it was just I and Luke, to a degree.

A memory that holds fondly nevertheless.

* Having re-read the manuscript in my printed proof copy (prior to publication and sale to the public) I should add that I believe the chronological order of meeting Sashi to be as is detailed in this chapter and the memory of Sashi teaching me to stop occurred latter but has, for whatever reason, been written in the previous one. I assign blame to my memory having faded with increasing old age.

CHAPTER FIVE

I must pre warn you that it all gets a bit tipped upside down from here on out. Well, for this chapter at the very least as I've yet to write the rest that follows, or edit and re-write.

From the advancement of Michael's visit to an unknown number of months onwards I and Luke had continued to skate in our little routine, continued to work at Zenos and life had been revolving in a constant circle completely and going round once more many times but alas at long last the circle had halted and the gears would finally grind to a halt. Times of change where upon us.

At some stage I and Luke had decided that we enjoyed our ice skating so much that we wanted to skate during the weekdays to get a little bit of practice in and just to add some more enjoyment into the week so we didn't have to wait so long in-between visits from Saturday to Saturday. Upon reflection at this point I had yet many lessons to learn in the workplace and common sense and maturity where two key areas of my personality that would need working upon. I say this because unlike many others whereby if they had a day of in the week then that's when they would have skated (in I and Luke's situation) but instead we both decided, egg'd on by each other, to take it upon ourselves to decide that we were better than Zenos and make our own schedule up. I had gone from the young professional in a suit eagerly attending work for the first time to an over confident in my position youngster about to embark on the very downward path that would take some time to climb again. Innocence, I had plenty of it. Although in my latter years is has enabled me to become a more rounded and professional individual so I do not look back with regret but rather meanwhile it was a bad decision it's one that inadvertently I've manage to use to set me on a more positive path.

The schedule that we would make had no pattern but simply involved both I and Luke phoning into Zenos will a call similar to "Sorry I cannot make it into work today I am not feeling well." With the phone call out of the way and work notified the details become somewhat sketchy but I can recall that it would be the case that both I and Luke would make our way towards the ice rink and spend the hours that we should be working and looking for jobs fooling around and listening to the rather dull music that played. The fooling around involved nothing more than: skating, taking videos and photos of each other and, to us, having a good time.

I fail to recall how long this went on for or how it came about but I think I must paint the entire picture rather than just the one of my negative youth and state that by this point the Zenos that we had joined was a far different one from that of the one we currently worked at. Georgina got out at the right time because beyond that it all went a bit downhill. There's only so many hours of lies sitting in an office having orders barked at you that you can take before you decide there's more to life and want a temporary out. It's no defence of course but I must add it because it's what I feel. Zenos is closed now so it's all a bit irrelevant to write but it's part of my history and story and forms a small part in the bigger picture so I can only mention what I feel relevant.

I remember the time three ex Zenos students appeared on the news slating the company and Iqbal, our tutor, made a big thing about defending the company and brainwashing us, somewhat, with a robot excuse by his employer to tell us it was all nonsense and we shouldn't play an ounce of attention. Not entirely relevant to anything but the company even while we where there were loosing grip of itself.

Short term I don't recall Zenos ever really pulling us up about our constant illness other than a short chat in the office upon return. I can safely say that we never returned saying "Alright girls we've just been ice skating, how was your day?" but rather learned how to play the game and judged how much time we could take off and when before it became suspicious. The business was full of young lads and I recall walking in many times to others getting somewhat of a talking to about whatever it is they'd done.

My downfall would eventually come and the jiggery pokery that I'd managed to work at Zenos would not work in the months that followed. In June 2012 I voluntarily left Zenos and Joined NCP.

If you drive or have visited any main city centre I would assume you've heard of NCP but in the interest of assuring we're all on the same page NCP is a privately run company that owns and operates car parks. I worked for NCP in Birmingham and at the time I believe they had around approx. 6-8 sites dotted around multiple locations.

My entry into this employment was somewhat in house and had already been set up. My interview was really a quick introduction chat and to confirm that I wanted to join the company.

Two weeks later when I started work I turned up on my first day to find that the manager that had interviewed me had been sacked along with four others on the suspicion of taking money. It would be fair to say that the first day was a somewhat nervous one and upon finding out the news I wondered if I'd still have a job to go into.

Five months later in November 2012 my past would catch up to me and I was sacked for not turning up for work. You guessed it, I'd phoned up as ill again and gone ice skating. There's a little bit more to the story this time.

I'd phoned one of the managers, Sied, and requested a day off which was not given to me. In being the absolute naive youth that I was I decided that just like at Zenos and with Luke many times before I would take the power into my own hands and give myself the day of and at the time thought nothing of it. Two days after zed phone call and halfway through a shift I was called into the office to sit down with one manager and one supervisor for a chat. I was sacked on the spot.

It was a hard lesson to stomach at first given that I'd never predicted the outcome back then but upon reflection it was a decision that worked out for me in the long run for the better, even if I did have to do some work to make it that way. Again just like with Zenos and to paint you the entire picture there is more to the story I need to tell you about.

NCP was not an enjoyable workplace nor was it an appropriate one for someone so young. I've not grown up in a bubble and so reality does not strike me much but I was subjected to all kinds of people crawling about on the top floor of those car parks at all hours of the day without anyone close by. Patrolling the car parks on my own I came across: drunks, druggies, teenagers, people having sex on the stairwells and on one occasion was chased down the stairs by a group of druggies after I'd told them to move on and leave. The stairwells smelt constantly of urine and had walls covered in blood that had splattered up when a druggie would inject the needle into their arm to shoot up and the needles would often be found lying around in all areas ready to infect you with whatever they could be carrying. It was often during any given patrol that you had to carry a sharps box with you as well as gloves, a litter picker and a bin bag. We were always told to be careful but beyond that we were left on our own to get the job done. A disgusting one that I'll never do again if it can be helped. I suppose you're only young once. And yes I did have to mop up the urine, paint and clean over the blood on the walls and remove the needles, condom packets and whatever else was found on the stairwells. I remember having to clean up after some party goers the one time after I'd let them stay for a short while longer because being friendly and giving them, somewhat, what they wanted was better than attempting to be an arsehole and stamping my feet plus with more of them than me and being several stories up with no one else around nor any CCTV I didn't dare risk trying to annoy drunk young lads who could quite easily hoist me over the side of the site and send me hurtling towards hard concrete to meet my maker. There was defiantly an art to getting the youngsters to do what you want. Many drug smoking youngsters from the nearby Matthew Bolton College visited quite regularly and I assume still do to this day because they've nothing else to do. The smell of weed flushes past my nostrils as I write this remembering the stench they all carried. Some were nice and one even offered me a drag while we chatted as I waited for them to finish smoking and leave but others and mostly were a pain in the rear that didn't want to move and were quite rude. I'm sure on a few occasions I had to call for backup from the older and more bulkier guys in an attempt to show them I wasn't going to budge easily and get them to do what I want. I was never assaulted thankfully but every shift when I was asked to patrol, on my own, the stairwells and several car park floors it would quite often be at the very front of my mind.

Another worthwhile note is that my father, whom had got me the job, had gone to work away in a different city for a few months and Sied had taken it upon himself in the lack of a defender for me to approach me one day while I was making my way from one car park to another to grab me and tell me that my job was being changed. It's a little backwards that I'm writing this here because this happened about half way through my five months at NCP. I originally joined NCP to work with my father on maintenance however as above had my job changed to a Customer Service Assistant, there was nothing formal, as you've read above, about the role at all. In reality Sied had it in for me and was a complete arsehole. The third person who worked on Maintenance was John and he didn't want to work with me because I was the brother of the girl that he'd cheated on and while the master was away John decided to take advantage of what he would never have got away with in front of my father and put a word in behind my back. Yes it was awkward working with someone whom I wanted to cave their skull in but I had been pre-warned during my interview that if anything was to take place I would be gone, in my defence I had some maturity and simply stated I was there to work not to payback the inconvenience that this boy had put my sister through. I dare to say it was a twisted situation but

I survived longer than John and got to watch the company rip the panels of his car in search of tools that he was stealing, or so they say, and he was sacked long before me. It's worth noting they had a habit of sacking people back then: Anthony the supervisor, the guy in the car who drove of angry and pissed off and caused a scene and many other youngsters who started during the same time as me but were gone before I was. Eventually even Michael (a different one from the Zenos lad) who I worked with at the time was sacked after me and probably many more in-between that I've forgotten about.

We're going to fast forward a little more here to November 2012.

It's at this point in the tale that we must say goodbye to Luke although in truth it had been quite some time since he had last visited. The reason, as far as I recall, was that he no longer wished to travel all the way from Northfield and had grown somewhat bored and no longer maintained the enthusiasm he once had. I don't recall there being one final text to call a day to all the good past times but rather a slow gradual decline that one day you blink and think "What happened there?" Luke's withdrawal did throw my future, for lack of a better word, into the unknown because without an amigo to skate with it was quite often the case that I would turn up on my own, skate round for a few hours and then simply leave without having talked to anyone, the temporary void gap between knowing no one to knowing everyone. In the interest of ensuring that I include all details of past mentioned affairs Luke, to my knowledge, didn't take his interest with Kerrie much further and eventually sizzled out alongside all the other possible romances and girls attention he gained along the way. In the area of Sashi I can only guess they remained friends. He remains close friends with and I think, possibly, works with Michael however we, I and Luke, for a long time, have had little to no contact. Friends, to my understanding, we remain.

Luke's decision to leave not only left me skating on my own for hour after hour but also meant that I had to suck up whatever enjoyment could be had while skating alone. It was this lesson that enabled me to continue on my own all the way up until November 25th 2012 when I became a steward.

CHAPTER SIX

Before I continue with a chapter about the era in which I was a steward I should like to mention one chapter worthy memory that occurred both before, played a part up to and continued shortly after I was a steward. I believe it fits in here in the grand order of chapters.

I, John, Caroline, Amy, Ryan, Joe and last but not least Georgie (no, not the same Georgie as I said goodbye to all that time ago). Quite a list of unknown names I hear you say, tis the new group of friends that for one period in time while just before and slightly after I was made a steward would attend the ice rink every Sunday almost religiously like I and Luke had once done. At this point in time days of attendance did not matter since I spent quite a bit of time at the rink and had nothing to do outside of the place but job search online. I should introduce you.

Joe and Georgia are brother and sister. Exception to the group because they skated on days few and far between mostly due to Georgie not wanting to attend without her brother by her side and Joe worked as a chef and therefore finding the time to visit was somewhat, he'd often remind us, difficult with the long hours he had to work. I didn't really know Georgie since she was quiet and then once she had found her feet she had a bit of a romantic spark with Ryan, who we'll get to, but beyond that I don't recall much about her. Joe of course I spoke to and knew quite a bit more.

John and Caroline are brother and sister. John was a steward for a period of time however due to, excuse me, dicking about on the ice and causing big chunks with funky stops that drove Kevin the manager crazy he was demoted, if that's possible, to a regular customer eventually. You could compare their friendship to the one between a rain drop and sun, it may exist however doesn't really last long before one of them gets the better of the other. Caroline was young at this point and very shy and quiet but eventually came out of her shell and as it turns out we got on quite well. We did have somewhat of a romantic spark for one period however it would eventually fizzle out and slowly we would lose contact. I feel sorry that such a young girl should have devoted such love and attention to me as she did at that point when I was more in love with the idea of a relationship that I was ready for one. I did the most respectable thing I could at that point and told her that I should like to remain friends rather than to play her along. We did for a long time, and as far as I'm aware, somewhat, do today but the spark went on for a while and it was all a bit more long winded than it should ever have been. I think in my defence I should like to write that the constant bullpoop that everyone spoke in my ear about her appearance at first and then god knows what else along the way I couldn't help but have my head crowded with everyone else getting involved. I don't think The Leisurebox was really the place for a relationship and I was far better off away from it than I was in it. I should add that eventually when she moved on and found a partner and is now respectfully and rightfully happy in a long relationship so I don't mean to re-write this in the hope that the spark may reignite but rather to recall and inform of the history.

Amy is someone who I recall watching skate around the ice rink during the popular era while attending with Luke and had ginger hair. She just used to skate around with her headphones in doing her own thing and latter, as my heart snapped into a million pieces, I would learn that all was not as it seemed and she was not a natural ginger. It did take me a while to recover from such awful news that was not broken gently.

Ryan studied at the same college as John and was a sound chap and as stated had a, for a short period of time, romantic spark with Georgie. I've seen him once since the rink closed at Solihull and we had a nice little catch up in the form of a short chat, nice to see an old friendly familiar face.

Introductions over with and time allowed for reflection I think this time period was the one in which I should have appreciated more than maybe I did at the time. I am of the opinion that, sadly, you cannot appreciate the time you spend with someone while it's going on and only when you look back and think about much latter on when everything's settled and it's all over. I feel that this group of people are particularly deserving of a chapter dedicated to the time we all spent together not only because it forms part of the story and would have been written regardless but also because the things that we did together and the times, conversations etc we had helped form me as a person and make me more rounded. I feel that my age at the time all this was taking place may describe why the memories are held with such tenderness and joy more so than I am able to explain in words.

There's no real formula or order to write the memories in so I'll jot them as they come to me.

The time we all sat on some seating in a square that's hidden around the back of buildings on Broad Street and alcohol may have been involved. The fact John made Caroline drink fruit shoot instead of alcohol because she wasn't legal age was cute at the time and stayed with me as a joke that I played for a short period. I may be recalling a slight memory of a nickname summoning here on my phone for her based around this but it's all fuzzy and inaccurate so I'll leave it at that.

The time we went to Bowlplex and took me on a trip down memory lane since it's where I and the group that I studied with at Zenos spent many happy hours socializing with alcohol while bowling, playing in the arcade and playing pool since it was only a short walk down the road from the back gates where the company was located. I playing pool with Caroline at the same table that I had sprawled across while drunk out of my face all that time ago, there is a picture of I and Wayne in this very moment somewhere. I recall I and Caroline flirting in the best way that we knew how and laughing at each other equally at just how bad we where at pool.

The time that on one of the visits to Bowlplex or in the area nearby we walked past a bus stop and I had quite the furious stand of with a man that was standing at the bus stop because he wouldn't stop staring at Caroline as we walked past. I think it annoyed me greatly that even when I looked at him to ask him to acknowledge that she was with me he continued gawping, a little bit of respect and I would not have minded, the fact that this thing could not accept that she was, somewhat, taken is what had annoyed me more than anything.

The time that John allowed Caroline to leave The Leisurebox alone with me for the first time and we spent some time in The Bullring together mainly window shopping. I recall offering to buy her a dress that she picked up and liked but she would not accept. I have a coat in the cupboard downstairs that she picked out and still it remains a favourite if not a little dated all these years on. I think this was a highlight in our time together since it was the first that we spent alone and could really be ourselves, I appreciated it greatly.

All the times we spent moaning while sitting in the warm room at how Sunday sessions were becoming more boring by the week since Kevin took over the playlist and decided to put music on that only people of whom had lived many years ago would have known. I like some Soul music and some old classics but this man's musical taste was beyond what someone of my generation could appreciate and thus became quite tedious. In fairness he did only put it on quite late in the day when everyone had gone but I think it might have drove us all to an early exit once or twice.

The time I saw Caroline for the first time in forever and sat opposite her in the cafe area not knowing what to do with myself because this was much latter on and she had got older and more attractive and I felt she was beyond what I was able to romantically catch, for lack of a better phrase. I think we spent some time bowling together alone, skated and then went shopping, maybe not in that order. Then Rob ruined it by asking me if I kissed her only moments after she left. I didn't, but maybe I should have. I probably should have taken her for dinner, I live and learn I suppose.

The time John let slip that he liked Amy but it didn't work out. Can't say I blame the chap when I, Caroline, Ryan and Georgie where all starry eyed in front of him. I think if four people where lovely dovey week in week out I'd want some companionship also. I think Joe might have been grateful that it didn't work out since he would have been sixth wheeling if it had happened. One for the record books I'm sure.

The endless amount of times I made Caroline jump by skating quite fast past her and performing all these little tricks and stops. She wasn't the greatest skater but certainly wasn't Bambi on ice.

That's all I'm able to recall, sadly. It seems anything else that occurred in our then social group has been forgotten. Simply because of my old age and bad memory, I should add. I recall everything I've written in this past chapter with fondness.

CHAPTER SEVEN

Small memories aside the time had arrived that for so long I had craved and lusted for. It was never my intention when we first visited to want to become a Steward but it seems that for me the path was written in my destiny that this would be the route that I would take to finally achieve my long set out goal of getting to know groups of people outside of Luke and form some new friendship groups. Ice skating is a social activity for the most part and while, as I've said above, Luke was never not enough three or more is certainty not a crowd, sometimes it's nice to branch of and sit with someone and then skate down the other end and have a chat with someone else and then branch of into the crowd and race after someone else you know for a few laps before you settle on the side barrier and tell each other how much older you've gotten since you last set eyes on each other and how much slower and how many less laps you're now able to complete as a result of getting old. Don't get old kids it's nothing but a trap.

November 25th 2012.

In truth it all seems so long ago however in memory it holds like yesterday. I often question where the time went and if it was all just really the best dream that I ever lived because it was over so fast I never really got to enjoy it to its full potential. Compare it almost to when you wake up five minutes before your alarm only in my version of things I never, ever, get to re-sleep or re-live those last five minutes as they're forever gone. I could spend forever hating the fact that it was sold and demolished purely because the land the building resided on was valuable in the modern age, more so than when it was constructed in the 1960's, however in my old age have to smile knowing that I got to live, in person with real sights, feel of the finger tips and smells, part of the old heritage of Birmingham that managed to survive longer than many of its counter parts constructed in a similar year.

Day dreaming aside, as lovely as it is and I could write in such a manner with every feeling I've ever felt for eternity, the small time gap pre becoming a Steward was a little annoying because I was Seventeen years old and therefore unable to sign on at the Job Centre. Ironically it has just struck me it would be this very place that would lead me post my Eighteenth birthday to the Job Centre once more.

After applying for many jobs and getting nowhere I decided to ask Kevin if there was any chance I could become a Steward. As above becoming a Steward was never my intention but it seemed a natural path to take if I wanted to continue skating and give something back to the place in return. I was ready to mature somewhat and wanted to make an investment in the place that had given me so much thus far.

I recall having to ask Kevin twice. First time I asked was to bring about the idea and propose the question and the second to see what the outcome to my proposal was after a bit of time being granted thus allowing Kevin to think about the idea. Thankfully somewhere along the timeline of which I am exactly unable to pin point the answer was yes and my fate was set in stone. It's all getting a bit "Get the tissues at the ready darling this is the emotional bit" that is if this were a movie.

I make no bones about pointing out the fact that it was this single decision that would save me in the long run when the money form NCP ran dry and would allow me to continue in this world that should the answer have been no then this world would have come crashing down and ended far before it had even developed into what it did. Words of thanks to Kevin and those involved in granting me Stewardship would not be enough. It paints maybe a more respectful picture of being a Steward than was true but I am grateful for the chance and hopefully I did not waste it, in their view that is, and yes their opinions do matter upon such a subject. Good old Kevin. Black coffee with no lid but instead I'd serve him with a lid of which led to many chasing around the cafe area and the ground level until he caught me and gave me a good kick up the bum. The joke never got old much to the amusement of Lee and Paul as they stood at the counter of the cafe drinking their Tea's with a live comedy performance running in front of them.

Beside the main character Kevin there was Iqbal. You could call Iqbal the unofficial manager since he not only spent so much time in the office but also had a voice of influence around the place and had used it in the delegation of my proposal of Stewardship. I would pinpoint the time in which Iqbal did such a thing was after the conversation that we had outside the ice rink one day at the very begging of getting to know one another and I assume a brief chat he knew enough to see that I was after more than just free entry and free second rate, at best, burger and chips every day of attendance. I'm always grateful that Iqbal went out of his way to help me in a time of need and I think that hopefully, somewhat, I managed to pay him back over the time up until the ice rink closed in our close and constant friendship. And hopefully, circumstances permitting, many more years dependent on events outside of my control that at the time of writing are currently on going.

I say I hope that I managed to repay him but the memory of our first conversation at the cafe counter when I wanted to redeem, so to speak, my first free drink springs to mind. It sticks with me that Iqbal would latter tell me that he thought that I would be rude but instead was shocked when instead unlike many other stewards before and after me I spoke with kindness and thanked him alongside being on the whole a polite individual.

My mannerisms may have been part of a greater plan to make good impressions upon everyone and based upon Iqbal the plan seemed to be going accordingly. Despite my saying it was somewhat planned it was more of an intention and yes me being polite was genuine and not an act, I did not for a moment forget where I had come from and where I now was but much rather that I had a standard to upkeep after being appointed a Steward.

The pay for being a Steward was free entry, one drink and one meal. Upon reflection it may seem like twopence but was better than rock bottom.

Background aside it would be a fair reflection to say that because of my background and approach to being a Steward I took it very seriously at first. Skating for four hours and not requesting a single drink nor meal beforehand. As time progressed this would change and I would eventually develop a habit of skating for an hour and a half and getting a drink and then another hour and a half latter would request the meal by means of keeping me going as skating at the best of times was a physical activity let alone the added responsibility of skating to teach, pick people up and guide them during their stay. I'm sure if I had the money I would have got through a lot more than just one measly plate of burger and chips. On the subject of money this perk of the job was just another in the long list of money saving techniques that would allow my last NCP paycheck to go on for as long as it did and was still ongoing at this point. Another small side note that I may wish to hide in font size one would be that I may have, once or twice, had more than one drink by means of keeping it on the hush hush. Cheers Iq.

It all got a bit opinionated at times for what it was

after all being a Steward was nothing more than turning up for four hours and helping out but then again what's to be expected when you give a bunch of sixteen to nineteen year olds a sense of power and responsibility and let them run free amongst each other, I guess we were inevitability bound to clash at some point. I guess I had maybe a more mature approach than others and it became after not very long at all that some people, Stewards, where simply in it, the game of being a Steward, for nothing more then free entry and wouldn't even bother putting on a Stewards vest for more than five minutes let alone actually be in the business of helping people in need of it and much rather could be found talking to friends all the while ignoring everything that was going on around them. Then again I shouldn't write too much into it because many people came and went within my time as a Steward meanwhile I continued on my carved out path none the wiser to their rise and downfall all a very small time-frame indeed.

Two memories stand out amongst them all. First was the one where I helped up a person larger than myself and we both tumbled with them on top of me and no one cared so I gave up the dramatic act of feeling squashed and limping around and second was the time a group of people of whom were all deaf came to skate. The one guy in the group I'd seen before but as far as I recall all the others would visit only this once so it must have been some form of group activity. The guy of whom name escaped me, if I ever did know it, called me over and wanted me to show him how to hockey stop and so to achieve this I had to communicate simply using my hands and body since I did not know sign language and they could not hear. It was somewhat challenging when verbal communication was not possible because trying to explain what side of the blade had to dig into the ice and how your weight and body should be positioned made it all that bit more difficult but I recall achieving it if only maybe slightly. I recall parting company with a smile and them trying out what I'd shown them.

Memories aside and time progressing I settled into being steward over the following months and found that to me it meant not only being able to enjoy a social activity and get out the house but also it felt like I belonged somewhere again. After an ill and false advertised job such as Zenos and then the foolishness that was NCP it was nice to find my feet in an environment where the majority of people that I was surrounded by where of a similar age and on the same page. Relaxing, ideal and appropriate. The right place at the right time I guess. As Grandad said much latter on something similar to "Everything happens for a reason" and "There's always something else you've just got to find it." I guess this was me after a shaky start to the working world finally taking the small steps to finding my place amongst it.

CHAPTER EIGHT

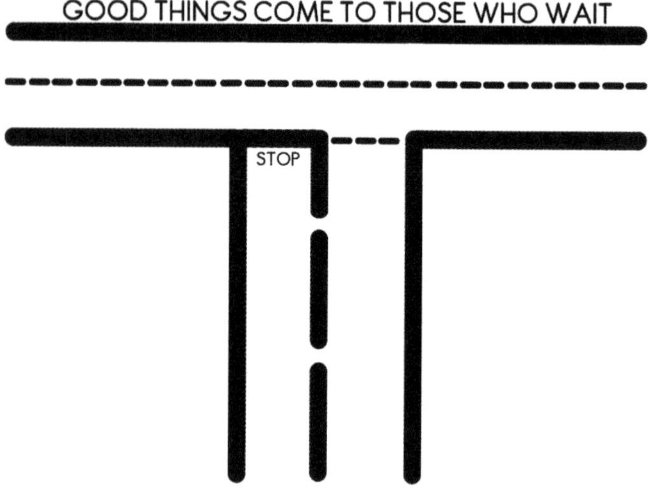

The months rolled on even further with November turning into December, Christmas came and went, Boxing Day, New Years Eve and finally 1st January 2013. Life continued as it ever had been for months to follow bringing us to just shy of the middle of the year in May 2013.

I had been living, somehow, on the last NCP paycheck all this time and both my luck and money were running dry. I wasn't desperate as such since I had a roof over my head and a place to go on weekends but I had been out of work for so long that I felt I needed a change and the money almost running dry had brought it home just that little bit more for me. I'd spent so long on cloud 9 (or is it 11?) that I'd just kept digging cautiously into the reserve bank when needed and hadn't, for a while, given it a second thought. I could have lived on free burger and chips for quite a bit longer and in this clouded reality but that wasn't the life I wanted for myself. As great as all this was I had decided within myself that I needed to pluck up the courage to ask if this would be my life or I was to move on. I needed to know if the place that I had fell in love with in 2012 and had devoted so much of my time to was to give me the full return and not only take me from a customer to a steward but furthermore allow it to become my career.

The man to ask was Colin. Colin had replaced Karen as the Rink Manager and Karen had replaced Manish. Chris was before Manish but had moved on before I arrived to manage Coventry. Manish was the best out of the lot. Karen stole and created her own downfall although god knows why Mike had to give her to us just to prove it was her that was stealing as she'd been evicted from another ice rink to this one on suspicion of the same thing. Months we had to endure her torturous nature and I got sent home once in the process because I told her young daughter I was incapable of making coffee and she found it inappropriate so an early release I got. I think you'll find, Karen, that it's inappropriate and unprofessional to have your little shits of kids running around the business you work for thank you very much. I may not know how to make a coffee and have spoken unprofessionally but at least I've never stooped as low as you for no good reason given that the money you were taking was done in greed, yuk! Is my disgust of this woman burning a whole into your page yet? Good riddance. Colin was alright. He certainly wasn't Manish but he wasn't a Karen and that was good enough.

So some day in May I pulled Colin aside and asked the grand question while quivering in my boots something to the effect of "Please sir, do you have a job?" while batting my eye lids giving him the.. oh no, wrong note.

I handed in my CV to reception and then a few weeks later asked if they'd had time to look through and consider it at which point I was invited for an interview.

I turned up all smartly dressed with the weight of the world on my shoulders and joined Natalie in the bar area. I remember one of the questions being "When you turn eighteen would you be willing to work in the bar?" to which I replied "Yes" in an attempt to make myself sound as appealing as possible. In reality and unknown to myself the answer could be been either yes or no and it wouldn't have mattered since by securing the interview I had in fact secured the job, although they wouldn't let on as much so easily. In truth I wouldn't even consider the entire event an interview but much rather a guided tour of the building explaining what was what and showing me where I would be working although again being a little innocent to it all I was still very serious about it all.

Another reason to appear serious about it all was because I wasn't the only person to be interviewed that day. Steph of whom was also a Steward and good friend arrived after me as we met at reception and I wished her luck as she made her way to the bar towards Natalie. Nor I or Steph knew how many jobs where available or how many people had attended interviews but afterwards once we had both been interviewed we met outside and happily to said to one another that if in the event that there was only one job available we would gladly concede defeat to one another and that there wasn't another Steward in existence more deserving of the opportunity.

Somewhere in-between the date of my interview and my start date, spoiler alert, I was stood outside the ice rink with Paul and Kevin amongst a few unknown others and Paul asked "Are you going to enjoy working here?" as I innocently responded

"If I am employed, of course" at which point Kevin then gave me a gentle nudge to say that Paul was attempting to give me an obvious hint to the fact that I would indeed be joining the company. Oh how innocent and blind to the obvious facts I was. A smile formed on my face and the rest of the day was history.

We both got the job for the record, I and Steph.

May 4th 2013 would be the start date of our employment.

In any other company it would have been a nightmare because as it turns out May 4th 2013 was a Saturday but at The Leisurebox the weekend was the prime time custom and therefore there couldn't have been a better time to start.

I recall Sashi texting me while I was sitting at the cafe tables signing all the paperwork and providing my bank details for payment etc. A little distracting but Sashi was worth the time even if it was a little unprofessional of me. Sashi encase for whatever reason you've forgotten was the female of whom all that time ago with Luke had taught me how to stop for the very first time and somehow in-between then and now had become a friend of mine. I'd always considered her special with fondness so the occasional check of the phone to see how far away she was didn't cross my mind as being out of order. Sashi wanted me to meet her outside to take her bag while she did whatever she was doing for the entire day only to then return latter and I assume the plan was to hang out, find out how the day had gone, talk and then to part company, it never happened like that. I recall walking out the front once but she wasn't there and then couldn't be bothered to again. Eventually she walked inside and after a quick hug and chat I took her things and she left. Her leaving would be the last that I would see of her on that day as despite my many hours of waiting she was far too busy doing whatever she was doing to return and instead I left her a text as to the location of her things and that was that. On the more fonder side of memories however she did text me the exact words "Good luck on your first day hope everything goes well I will prob see you later :D xxx" so at least that's something. The only person to do so and was unexpected so provides a little insight as to why I considered her special. Many young girls that visited the ice rink wouldn't have had the brain cells to rub together and realise that such a small gesture could mean so much.

With Sashi gone and the paperwork signed and our posts assigned I would start work on the Bowling area on the ground floor.

The first shift I worked with Shenila and Raffina. I don't recall how it exactly started but I probably got a brief introduction before I made my way up the all mighty step to head behind the bowling counter. As a customer you don't really think much of it but I have a strong but vivid, ironic I re-

aisle, memory of walking cautiously and waiting before being welcomed up to the counter as I was a little hesitant and naturally still adapting to being able to do all the things that working for the company now enabled me to do. Both the girls walked me through the basics and showed me what was what: how the shoe numbers worked, how to set up games, how to fix problems, how to greet customers so on and so forth.

I quickly learnt that customer service in this role was key as the customer was often the most challenging aspect. It wasn't that the customer was always right it was more that after changing lanes about a handful of times people reached their limit and often requested refunds. I loose count of how many times I'd have to call for a manager while observing a conversation out the corner of my eye of them receiving a long and detailed account of what had happened and all that the person had been through during their stay when little did they know it was probably the hundredth time the managers had heard it that shift. The result of this conversation was often a refund and a free game on top although it would only take up several more hours of the customers day so often was refused. I should say that the above observation and opinion was formed over my entire stay than just on the first day alone. It comes as no surprise, to me at least, that the good old saying "They give out so many refunds how do we even make money?"

springs to mind and well often did we ever?

Several months down the line is all it took, at the risk of sounding over confident, to get used to bowling to the point that I was the first and only person in the mornings effectively opening and setting everything up. Often it was the case that one person would turn up when we opened and then the next would start a few hours later and then they would overlap with the afternoon to close person. The middle shift was the worse because some people, mentioning no names, had a habit of not turning up, for ever evolving reasons, and therefore "Can you work till close?" was often asked and you'd need a good reason to not be able to. Finish and escape to the pub became key after a while. The aforementioned setup involved nothing more than pressing a few buttons on the computer to get everything set in motion while the machines worked themselves up to temp and any problems became obvious. Tell a lie: flicking the switches on the wall to test all the lights, turning the music on, unknotting all the shoe laces, spraying some shoes, visiting the toilet a billion times waiting for us to open, dancing to the music, making noises down the radio, watching the vending machines thinking why anyone bothers to put money into them when no one ever wins any prizes out of all but the teddy bear one, escaping and hiding out of sight of the CCTV to the back of the cafe with Iqbal only to receive a call from the manager watching the cameras asking us to get back to our station and probably a whole lot more that I forget. Talking of Iqbal I recall quite often when it was quiet he would come over to help out and then return when a customer arrived at the counter. We all had to be fit and multi-talented to survive as we were all, at times, stretched to our limits. Bowling's limits was not having enough staff on a busy day and trying to get through it with only two people, oh to be young again, probably the only reason we ever did it.

Dreamland aside, again, the first shift wasn't really nearly as difficult as I'd expected and was over before it had really begun. In reality I and Steph where put on the rota for a four hour stint to ease us in and see how we got on in the thick of it all. Personally I was glad to be back working and earning and even more so given that it was in The Leisurebox of all places that I'd finally landed on my feet.

Once the shift had ended I and Steph decided to skate, since it was Saturday so why not, but found ourselves to be tired so only did so for a few hours compared to our usual most of the day as a Steward. In truth I was waiting for Sashi to turn up and kept looking at the double doors hoping that at some point she'd burst through them but sadly she never did, much to my annoyance.

Eventually I and Steph called it a day and left together as we'd done many times as Steward's since we both walked the same way back. We parted ways with her heading into Moor Street Station and I continuing down Moor Street Queensway towards my bus stop located by the abandoned Toys R Us.

A blink of an eye latter I would arrive home and it was all over. Well, the first day at least. Only another 365 days before it would be over for good.

CHAPTER NINE

May 25th 2013.

A whole twenty-one days after my first shift I turned eighteen years old, seems Natalie didn't have to wait long for her wish of getting me to work in the bar, or at least being eligible to do so, for long. Many people consider their eighteenth birthday to be a special occasion: 16, 18 and 21. The key to the door and all the rest of it. Natalie would be amongst those people and she did offer me the day of but the reality was that I'd only end up turning up anyway and so as not to want to taunt my fellow new colleagues I asked for a reduced shift and hours of my choosing so I could enjoy the day in all its entirety. My wish was granted although I doubt Natalie or others understood why I wanted to work at all.

I'm not really a big fan of birthdays and avoid the limelight where possible so considered the day to be like any other and it wasn't until out of the blue Matt and Josh burst into skate hire with me standing at the front somewhat confused as they made their way down the isles to the back laughing amongst themselves and telling me that I wasn't allowed back there so I had to confine myself to standing in front of customers waiting to be served apologising for not being able to do so. Eventually the call arrived and the coast was clear for me to serve customers again and as I grabbed a pair of skates and made my way into the alley way between the racks the skates where kept in I found blue balloons with eighteen written on them, in white writing, tapped to the end and I think a banner. A gesture out of the blue that took me by great surprise and I was truly grateful for.

The mischievous duo was far from done with their antics or me. After I finished my shift, as usual, I went to skate only for them to insist that I must have two of these balloons tied with one on each hip. I didn't mind but I think others, customers, may have done so. The rink was still at half capacity divided by the big curtain and blue matts and on this particular day was shortened even further by some cones that ran across the bottom third of the ice rink due to a burst pipe. I can only assume there must have been debate over if to open the ice at all because it was a tight squeeze once everyone, customers and regulars, started to flood onto what little space they could find. By the time I arrived laced up and ready to go I must have hit probably nearly just about everyone at least once on my many laps round. I didn't hold on the balloons for long mind given that others: friends, stewards etc where more enthused by the idea than I was so took them from me to skate with for themselves.

Eventually I called it a day and decided to stop by the middle barrier for a rest and in doing so would spark the first conversation between I and Sophie. Sophie was a friend, in the past, of Kerrie and Sashi and was one of the last old timers that I had yet still to speak to. Well, the ones that still visited that is. I recall not what the conversation was about nor how long it lasted but here's her introduction. At the time a fresh faced youngster that I knew absolutely nothing about but all being long over I'll round it up as more headache memories than peaceful ones. I'm sure there's more to write and maybe I will in small doses but for now I'll save setting your page on fire again.

After I and Sophie's brief but for once pleasant encounter, oh the days, I decided it was time to make my way downstairs where I met Matt and Josh in the bar area. It wasn't ever in my plans for the day to get drunk it became quickly clear to everyone but I, since I was in anything but an ok state, that I'd already achieved it after probably not many drinks at all. My first alcoholic drinks not only went down but they'd soon be coming back up if I didn't have something to eat. Thankfully Iqbal was on scene running back and forth to the cafe to enjoy the experience just as much as everyone else and on one of his many trips he delivered a premium plate of burger and chips to help sober me up and line my stomach. Lesson from the old wise man kids, if you ever drink alcohol ensure you've eaten before you do otherwise lord help the stumbled confused state you'll soon fall into. By this time we'd all moved from the bar and onto the bowling lanes: Sean, Matt, Josh, Iqbal, Jade and a friend of Sean's. Jade worked down in the office doing accountancy while Ruth, Big J's mom, was away on maternity and Sean I'll properly introduce in two chapters time.

From the bowling lanes back to the ice rink I recall leaving the half eaten chips and burger on the side thinking "Someone else will get that" and then making my upstairs. You could question, as any sane person might, if skating drunk was a good idea and to that I say "Almost definitely. This would be my first time skating drunk although I'm not quite sure that the managers knew that I was or if they'd of allowed it if they did but either way this encounter would spark many more drunk skating sessions to come. There was no fast and hard rule against people skating drunk but only that alcohol was not allowed upstairs although as time progressed I recall that being somewhat relaxed providing they were not causing trouble. My reason for saying definitely is because while I've no idea what I looked like to everyone else I managed to: enjoy the music more, skate faster and end up in my own little world. In truth I probably looked like a red faced (since alcohol gave me alcohol flushes that gave me a red face) fool but I enjoyed myself and that was that.

After probably not a very long skate at all I, Matt and Josh made our way outside of the ice rink through the double fire doors towards the square part at the top of the ramp. This would have been, in the past, where the ticket office or entry to the ice rink was but all that resided in this small square nowadays was blue matts and rubbish. We sat on the matts watching the traffic and life go by as we, or they, drank beer from the cans and let the day waste away. Regrettably I'd decided in my drunken state that walking across hard concrete floor and outside in ice skates would be a good idea however soon found upon my return to the ice after our adventure that I'd damaged them for good. Long live the Bauer Vapour TI's, 2012 – 2013.

With the day over with and myself a little more sober I called it time to go home. One thing that I'd done while bowling with the group, or rather not stopped doing, was looking at Sean's friend, Kayleigh. I've no idea if it was the alcohol but at that point in time she was the best looking thing in the world and I was on cloud 9 (or is it 11?) and being my birthday I decided it was a good idea to try my luck. Spurred on my comments made by Jade such as "She keeps smiling so that's positive" or something similar my world would come shattering down when at the end of the day before I'd got a chance to make a fool of myself Sean and Kayleigh parted the ice rink together without me as two people of whom had suddenly developed a romantic interest in one another. The best news was yet to come in that the days that followed I would find out that they'd both woken up and realised what they'd done and mutually agreed it was better that it continued no further. So, even if I did fail to romantically attract Kayleigh's attention the satisfaction of having a friend attempt to grab her from under my nose on my birthday only to then fail a matter of a day or two latter outweighed my still intact relationship status of single. Gingers 1 – 0 Sean.

CHAPTER TEN

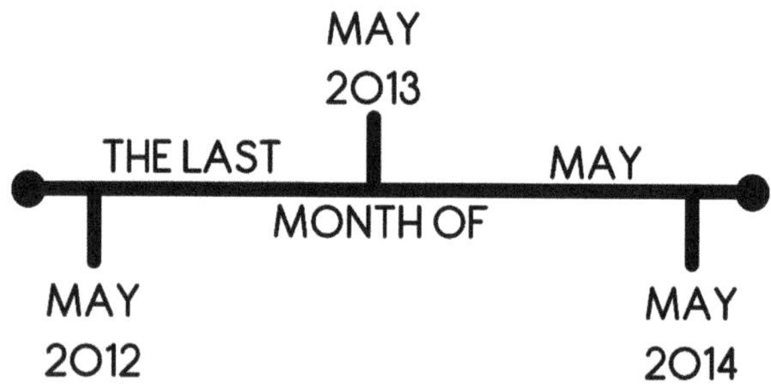

May 26th - May 28th 2013.

I don't have an exact date sadly and if you don't mind I'd rather not look through all the texts, images etc to find out given that it will only enable me to find many forgotten pieces of material that I'd much rather reside to history and the back of my mind so I'll insist that we leave it to the three dates outlined above.

Two facts. Fact one – it was only days after I turned eighteen. Fact two – it would be the last time that I would see Sashi in person. The first sets the significance of such an age that events unfolded and the second sets out in plain sight the fatal blow.

There was nothing particularly special about this day at the start of it nor while I was living through it in truth. It started out like any other and ended like any other: I awoke, went skating, came back and that was that. It was only much latter on after events had unfolded that I started to remember this day with fondness and hold the pictures that where taken of I, Sashi and Joe together with some affection.

It's all a bit confusing given that it seems I've written this down a thousand and one times and yet searching this manuscript for the word Sashi there's no mention of her, or very little, beyond this chapter to the point that pre this edit I had not fully concluded the story. I can forgive myself for this oversight in that in truth since I'd not fully accepted the entire satiation and series of events that followed this day and therefore could not have possibly provided closure when I had not yet accepted it in myself. I was a broken man attempting to talk about, with discretion, a period in time that was very hard to live through indeed.

On the day in question I had attended the ice rink as usual on my day of and had the attitude that whomever I would bump into would be whom I'd spend the day socialising with. It wasn't uncommon during holidays, half terms etc that we'd all congregate on random days at the rink and go with the flow. Some days you'd bump into JB and Big J and others it would be Sean and other regulars. Today would be the day that finally I would bump into Sashi and Joe. Twenty two – twenty four days after Sashi had sent me the text that she'd soon return she finally appeared. Gents, if a lady ever tells you she'll be ready in five minutes be prepared to wait as long as it takes. We, all three of us, spent the day sitting around, talking, skating and taking photographs. The day seemed like any other and after a catch up and an enjoyable day we parted company as normal until next time (the sad fact being, as of 2nd July 2017, there hasn't yet been a next time).

What I'm really trying to get at, write, type and have been avoiding for so long is that months after this day I would text Sashi and ask her why she'd not been around and at first she would respond with the truth but the white lie truth in that she had back pain. It was true enough but it wasn't the full extent of what really was the reason behind her not being around. You have to understand that this is someone that from the first time I had laid eyes upon I considered special and then become very good friends with only for her to then vanish and not re-visit without any obvious reason and so naturally I was curious and wanted to see her again. I text her one day while sitting in skate hire with Big J after a conversation we'd had and he'd convinced me to just talk to her. She soon responded and a grin, that wouldn't last long, grew on my face like no other. Over the period of time that followed I, sounding selfish here, went through one of the most shaping experiences of my life in that what had happened is that Sashi had developed cancer. I say selfishly because whatever pain, tears, anger and so on I had could not even come close to what she was going through. There was many dark days of crying at work, breaking down in the back of skate hire punching the wall and work mates standing around not knowing what was wrong or what to do, days of talking to Rob with him asking what was wrong and all I could say was "There's a good friend that's ill and I can't do anything about it, it's the worst feeling in the world." I couldn't tell anyone she had cancer because she'd made me promise, for her sake I assume in the interest of privacy, but in truth and upon reflection all this did in the long run was damage me even more. I was so, in my view, loyal that I didn't tell anyone at first until Sean somewhat beat it out of me after he could see that something was wrong and I wasn't my normal self. It felt so horrible to tell him because despite the fact Sashi and Sean were good friends also I felt like I'd betrayed her. I think Raffina was the only other person I ever told, reluctantly. Keeping it hidden for so long created so much pain, anger and emotions that I had no idea how to control that it probably hasn't done my any good in the long run. I've no idea why it hit me so hard but I think it just demonstrates how much I cared at the time. I'd lost a teacher, Mr Gardiner, before while in year ten at secondary school to cancer so it was nothing new to me but I think it was this past experience that taught me just how much I didn't want to lose her. I offered many times to bring her flowers and whatever else since she was only a few miles outside of Birmingham City Centre at Queen Elizabeth Hospital but she never accepted my invite and said that it was best that I stay away and that it was family only that could visit. I often fell into a state of dream about this situation and imagined myself sitting on a bench outside the hospital while throwing stones at a window only for Sashi to appear and we'd smile at one another while I had a bunch of flowers, to show I'd kept my promise, and eventually depart leaving the flowers on the bench. In truth I never attempted to visit not once, I can't tell you how I feel about that in truth but please believe it was not an easy decision to make in the slightest.

I could go on and on but the painful conclusion is that one day in my very emotional state I sent her a text telling her that she was the only person that I'd ever loved and didn't want to lose her. This text then sent her into the polar opposite of the person I'd known and suddenly she was texting me telling me she needed space and that she didn't need all this contestant messaging and me telling her that I loved her. I regret to say that I said "Yes" when she asked "Love, what as friends because I really don't need all that right now?" when in truth I should have grew a back bone and told her I meant what I'd said but the fear of losing her was huge so I lied, a white lie I'd like to think in the best interest of hopefully keeping in contact with her.

Eventually she turned into a sour grape and stopped talking to me all together. All the conversations we had happened on WhatsApp and I still have. She put status up such as "If you haven't got my new number take the fucking hint" and so on and so forth and of course I didn't have her new number and couldn't help but feel like I was the aim of the message. I shouldn't consider myself so special given that Aaron of whom I cannot recall right this second when he comes into play would latter tell me that Sashi had done the same thing to him only that two males had messaged him telling him to keep his distance from her. I didn't get any threatening messages from anyone so that's something. My biggest fear for a long time was that this story would out and I'd be ruined somehow but I'll put that down to my anxiety.

25th December 2014 would be the last day that I

would talk to her. I've just quickly opened the Facebook messages and I recall that after many months of not being able to take the silence I message her asking why we were still friends on social media given that it seemed like she wanted nothing to do with me. It was basically me wanting to know if I was deleting her, by removing her from facebook, out of my life for good or if there was something beyond this black hole of no contact. There's some friendly messages that follow talking about meeting up and we soon clicked back into our old ways but nothing has ever come of it. Two years later and I hold no ill feeling but rather I'm glad that I've finally, at long last, gotten it written down and out of me so that I can move on.

To Sashi,

I'm sorry that the world has to acknowledge your unfortunate and unpleasant situation that seems to have happened so long ago but I ask you to understand that for so long I carried it around on my shoulders like a weight full of emotion I had no idea what to do with. Finding out someone, one of your friends who you cared about madly, could be taken from you without being able to do anything on the other side of a phone screen miles away was harder for me to cope with than I can ever express in any piece of writing I produce. I've only written about it after so long because I feel it forms a vital part of the story and cannot, for any longer, go unsaid. For so long I've attempted to remove, hide and forget about it like it was never a part of my history but the truth is, and I realised this only days ago, is that it happened and that for the rest of my life, like it or not, this will stay with me. As much as I've tried, and believe me I've tried, it's not going to go away and not talking about it doesn't help anyone.

I'm glad that you're ok, I believe at least, but don't appreciate the way that things ended. Well, somewhat ended. It wasn't exactly nice to go through all that to then hit a brick wall and suddenly loose contact with you. I shouldn't make this all about me and I can only apologise for saying I loved you and can't for a second begin to contemplate what must have occurred on your side when you read the message but I ask that you understand I meant not for it to create ill feeling between us and only that I wished to care and be there for you. I've no idea if bringing all this up again will create more ill feeling or what but what's done is done.

I hope one day even for a moment we might be able to sit amongst one of the many cafes that line Birmingham canals together on a warm summer's day and remember it all. All I'm saying is that I don't think any less of you for not talking to me and upon reflection, and there's been much of it, I didn't at first think about how hard it all was for you because I was so caught up in every emotion possible. I understand, as best as I can and want to, your decision and thank you for providing closure by greeting my Facebook messages with some kindness. Even if we shall never set eyes upon one another again I would like you to acknowledge that meeting you was indeed the best experience of my life and I'm sorry that you of all people, given how kind and all the rest of it you are, had to go through such a thing.

I will admit that as a result of all this I have trouble saying the word love. I can't say it and mean it. You'd say something like "Stop being silly" but as you've said yourself before I'm of the old romantic type and therefore can you really ever love more than once? I've said it, used it and meant it but will there ever be another love? A rhetorical question only fate for the remainder of my days can answer.

I kept the photographs from that day we took together on my phone and made backups on the computer, I've no idea where they are though, because despite my many attempts during the dark void of no contact to remove you from my life in anger I just simply could not go through with it. I wrote a book too. It's more of a little diary about everything that went on not long after it happened. I've no intention of writing what's in it since just as your cancer was a secret the diary is mine trapped with it the feelings, emotions and I wrote how I felt and what happened. It's nothing magical nor extensive and contains no more than a few chapters but it's enough it bring it all back when I'm at my computer from time to time and find myself opening it and reading through it. I called it "*Limited Time 1 – The Lasting Memory*" and there's a picture of the front cover design on my Instagram somewhere amongst all the photos. I, at first, did want to publish that book along with a second one about Iqbal and then more and more about every person that I knew but after yours I couldn't write anymore and so this is how this memoir, autobiography or whatever you'd like to call it come about. I'm not saying you're the reason this entire manuscript of at present 45,000 plus words and growing exists since the countless number of hours I've spent moulding it was all my doing but I thank you for helping me realise that not only do I enjoy writing but I enjoy writing about the times of which I've lived through since it's what I know best and feel I can write about without exaggeration when not needed.

Towards the end of The Leisurebox I remember walking around with Raffina and I, in not so many words, told her that I was glad that the place was being demolished because it was the only way that I could put this chapter of my life to bed. Walking around the place without you and having visual flashbacks of what went on, the first time we met and the many hours we spent talking together, was, in the end, too much to go through constantly and eventually felt it affecting my work. I questioned leaving but I could never bring myself to do it. I never mentioned you but much rather said that there was simply too many painful memories in this place and it had to go. I miss the place of course but I have to agree with my former self in that life's worked out ok since so it certainly wasn't for the worse.

I could write countless letters each containing thousands of words and each differ from the other. I've no real idea what I want to say to you or how to say it or if there's a time or a place for me to say anything at all but here's my one attempt that should this go any further than my external hard drive, in the form of print on the mass market, shall be remembered and read by the general public and hopefully remembered, to some degree, in history.

It's a tiring thing this whole experience.

Life's short, thank you for being a part of mine.

With Love (as friends),
Ginge

CHAPTER ELEVEN

To introduce or not to introduce, that is the question. Well, I've already told you a little about Sean so I'm not really sure how much there is left to say. The answer? A whole lot. If you could look outside the book and envision how things used to be to how they are now you'd question how it would be possible for two people to go from being so close to drift so far apart but such is life.

Sean. A small man, boy, thing that liked alcohol, lots of, and violence. When we first met he was quite serious about martial arts, I forget what form he practised, and I recall a few occasions whereby he'd run for the bus and leave me behind because not going was almost like a sin but as time progressed he became more about the visits to McDonalds and hanging out at The Dragon Inn than anything else. He was quite into his music as well but over time that faded too. I'm not painting a negative picture for the fun of it just how I saw it decline over the time I knew him. Well, what I knew of him. I don't think Sean is the type of person that you ever really fully know in truth. Liked: singing, guitars and girls. We shared some mutual interests and spent many happy hours together but we're two different people that managed to merge together for a summer or two.

The first memory sticks with me because of the funny faces it makes me pull at every time I re-encounter it in my mind. Now I'm not going to join the ever popular group of growing people that like to claim they've got a condition because it's the cool thing to do but at this point in time I was very particular indeed about hand washing and what I would and wouldn't touch. OCD like but not diagnosed shall we say. On the day in question I was working a bowling shift with Sean when Kevin approached and asked us both, since it was quite quiet, to clean the balls and serve the customers as and when they came. Directed to the small, dirty and horrible smelling room that was the cleaning cupboard that gave me the creeps every time I had to go in it we were shown what had to be used and how the job was done. I would rinse and Sean would clean or vice versa, simples. We eventually worked out a method that got through it as fast as possible but it was a never ending task that in truth you could never win. Watching paint dry was genuinely more effective because it had a positive outcome set in stone whereas cleaning bowling balls only guaranteed that you'd put a fair bit of elbow grease into a job that didn't give you anything in return. The bowling balls had been damaged, marked and dirty for so long that we needed new ones for it to ever become a reality of getting them clean. The ironic thing was that, and I'm not sure how close to the end we are in days, when the end did arrive cleaning out the room at the end of the lanes I watched Andy pull out endless amounts of shiny bowling balls and wondered why we'd never had the common sense to put them on the racks instead of the old, used and grubby ones all that time ago. I think Kevin wanted to give I and Sean a long wait and a glass hammer as an early Christmas gift. With as many bowling balls done and cleaned as possible we shut up shop and returned behind the counter for a long earned rest. That was the first time I did the job and every other time it arose I did everything in my power to dodge it. Never again.

Task aside it was in that brief encounter and memory that I first come into contact with Sean. Before that I'd viewed him as nothing more as the new kid that I used to watch linger behind the others in skate hire hiding away and not really doing much talking. That soon changed I tell the.

Months in advance with what many others had branded a bromance I and Sean arranged our first night out together. The taste for alcohol on my eighteenth birthday had left me with wanting more and as Sean liked to go out clubbing and had more experience I considered it a smart move to ease myself into the nightclub and pub scene slowly as to see what I was comfortable with. Sounds naff but I hadn't had many social experiences up to this point where alcohol was involved beside my times at Zenos and surrounded by people I didn't know whom weren't in control of their actions I went with the side of caution.

In the interest of doing things for the first time this would be the first time in a long time that I'd sleepover at someone's house since I was a child. Well, in truth even back then the person had stayed at my house rather than I at there's. This whole non diagnosed OCD thing again I'm afraid. The idea of waking up without my creature comforts of a warm shower, toothbrush, toothpaste, face cream where I'd left it, my own pillows, blanket, books by my bed etc just seemed alien. Well, I say books but that's more now rather than then but the picture I've painted should enable you to join the scene as it was.

It took Sean some convincing to get me to stay over rather than return home in a taxi, I've no idea why he wouldn't let me, but once it was done and set in stone he had a smile about him. I've no idea if bringing someone home was a big thing to him as to show of the flat he lived in with his father but both Sean and his father viewed it as the more sensible decision vs me going home drunk in a taxi. I guess we'll never know if I would have hailed a black cab and ended up taking out a loan to pay for the fare, the mind wonders. I will admit that while I forget what it looks like his dad did have a nice road pedal bike. A small but very manly man cave.

On the night in question I and Sean made our way via bus from Birmingham City Centre to Moseley on the No. 50. Once we'd reached a destination a million miles away we arrived, after a short walk, at his flat and changed into our going out clothes. Then out the door, again, quickly and a walk down the road, a very long road to me, to the places he'd planned to take me. One thing that I had overlooked was my going out attire, more particularly the shoes. I've no idea what ones I deemed sensible to wear but I soon got a talking to about how I might not even get let in on the door because of my choice. I did but I defiantly made a note as to what would be acceptable next time based on what others were wearing.

When we arrived inside the group was: I, Sean, Julian and Paul. Julian was, and is, Sean's father and Paul we've already talked about. The guy who stood outside and told me I'd get the job but I missed the hint in plain site, remember? A small group but this was more of a casual night out rather than a big piss up on the weekend. Paul and Julian had been friends for longer than a number I am able to count up to and so that's how they met. I recall many comparisons on the night how I and Sean were the mini version of Julian and Paul. I slightly remember, amidst the bottle after bottle of alcohol, that there might have been more friends of Julian there but I was more confined to the small area by the bar sitting on the back of a sofa than I was about meeting new people and small talk.

If ever there was a birth spot about the long running joke that was my bad dancing, or rather lack of, this would be it. Confined, by my own choice, to this small area my dancing reached as far as a head nod and that was about it. I'd not danced in my life and I'd not needed to. Sure we all like music but the idea of shaking your stuff on the dancefloor while alcohol flows around you amongst people you've never met before was an alien idea. The bright flashing L.E.D's was enough to throw me off guard and the only move I'd have pulled, if I'd have tried, was the worm to get to the front door and some fresh air since I wouldn't have been able to find my way back to my feet amongst the large crowds and constant blinding effect. Overtime we'd discover that I had zero natural rhythm and the head nod was my sole jam.

With the booze blurring most of the night out the next part was the leaving or rather lack of wanting to. I think it must have been throwing out time and so Sean decided for me that it was better that we headed home to his flat rather than continue a night out on the town. In truth I'd gotten a taste for it and wanted to go elsewhere with Julian but Sean, as far as I recall, had things to do the next day and it was past his bedtime. I had no choice but to turn back and watch the nightlife fade as I walked down this road I cared not for towards a flat I wasn't ready to receive. The night was young and so was I, bad decision I'd say even today.

I can only say that the long walk that I'd endured on the way to the bars was made even longer on the return trip by the contributing factor that was with alcohol in my system everything was, or seemed at the time, so brilliantly bigger. Walking took much longer and the world required so much more investigation. I found myself wondering up to trees and inspecting the leaves for detail talking to Sean about things I was observing and how brilliantly wonderful they were. After I was done talking and he wasn't listening I then ended them with a wonderful karate kick to demonstrate my martial arts, or rather lack of, skills. We made some home videos and I've watched one or two since. I can't make sense of them for the life of me given they contain nothing but random chatter and laughing. Sean performs some moves in the road, handstands or whatever else, and somehow we manage, amongst all this, to not only not come into contact with another human but avoid getting run over. I say that because most of our time was spent dancing amongst the roadside. The tarmac seemed so attractive.

Like I'd been run over I awoke with daylight in my face and Sean needing me out the flat for me to leave with him to head the way we'd just come and separate ways in town. A banging headache and feeling rough as is humanly possibly I took another bus home and upon arrival slept it off. What a sight I must have been for people waking up and heading out on their daily commute first thing in the morning.

CHAPTER TWELVE

21st September 2013.

I hope the dates correct. JB's Birthday.

If there's one thing that JB was known for it was that he knew how to have a good time and ensure that those around him did too. Around the ice rink he'd create an atmosphere of hyper energy and a buzz that came along with it. Not everyone understood or appreciated, at times, the level of hyperness that he carried around with him but as far as parties where concerned at least he knew how to host a good one.

Kind enough to invite me to stay at his house in West Bromwich to make it easier on me in terms of travelling I reluctantly accepted. I only say reluctantly because the only other time I'd stayed at someone's house was with Sean and that was a few miles outside of town not a whole different city. I'd travelled to and from Wolverhampton before many times via the tram line so wasn't totally uncomfortable with the idea of how to get to West Bromwich but anxiety got the better of me and I made a bigger deal of the entire trip than was ever needed.

I took the bus into town and then the tram to the name of the stop that he'd text me earlier in the day. Once I'd gotten of the tram the level of anxiety only increased and I had to somewhat force myself to stay rooted to the spot instead of running away and catching the tram back to Birmingham. The platform quite literally on the opposite side was as far as I needed to go to get back but somehow in my state of panic it seemed like a million miles away. The fact that JB wasn't responding to my texts only made things worse and eventually Jamz would appear and guide me through the many back roads to JB's house. I was beyond glad when Jamz arrived because the many people including two rough looking guys in particular didn't really sit well with me at the tram station and I'd kept my eye on them throughout the entire time I stood there to see what they were up to. I escaped unscaved thankfully but the night was only just begging and I couldn't have been more out of my comfort zone if I'd have tried.

Arriving I encountered a large group of males sitting on the wall outside the house and crowded around the front door. A group of JB's friends that where more natural to the area than I was and like a duck out of water "Excuse me" and "Thankyou" was about the only phrases I managed to produce in my haste to get past them and in to the house. These friends made lads in Birmingham that think they're something look like ants that's for sure. There's a different way of life and I was just glad I was here on personal business rather than getting lost in the wrong area. Needless to say that once inside I was in no hurry at all to leave without the guided escort of JB and the people that I knew inside.

The room I entered was the first on the left, the sitting room. I recall the other rooms with some detail as the layout of the house sticks in my mind like it was only yesterday. Shortly after the first door there was a second on the left of which was Elijah's bedroom then walking down the hallway some more and there's a mini sitting room and then beyond that right at the back of the house is the kitchen. Upstairs was a bathroom at the top on the right and then two bedrooms. I recall a cupboard possibly located on the landing area and maybe a fourth door upstairs although those are faded and probably not true memories. I never went outside although recall the door that led to outside was in the mini sitting room downstairs.

Once inside the only person that I didn't recognize was JB's brother. Still to this day all the years latter I've no idea if they really are blood related but that's how they referred to each other and that's what I believed, whom am I to argue? Why would I argue? Others inside the room where: Elijah, Jamz, JB and a friend of ours from Tamworth that had come down to celebrate also, Alex I think was his name although I'm not one hundred percent sure nor can I find him on social media so we'll go with that. Elijah I believe was related to JB but again my memory is somewhat faded. Two females were also present although again the fuzzy state doesn't enable me to recall if that was before or after the pub. Alcohol has a lot to answer for.

My introduction with JB's brother was quite a challenging one and it came about since when I arrived at the house JB had his PS3 connected up to a little TV in the sitting room and was playing the then newly released GTA V. JB's brother took exception to the fact and decided to challenge my announcement that I'd finished the story mode of the game only after a couple of days of it being released. I didn't state that I'd completed it one hundred percent but much rather just the single player missions. I had pictures on Instagram of the credits taking in my bedroom clearly showing it wasn't a random picture from google but no one believed me. The brother asked me what the ending of the game was and after I gave my answer he still didn't believe me and told me what actually happens of which a noise erupted between JB, Jamz and his brother like there was a trio of judges against my claim. In truth there was actually three different endings to the game but I had no time to voice reason and instead was crushed. When it all went quiet again and I'd found a corner of a sofa to curl into it was time to set out for the pub. We'd all had pre drinks at the house so beyond this point the memories are fuzzy.

When we arrived at the pub the security guard on the door was one of the lads that in the past had worked at The Leisurebox and so naturally I recognized him. Not on talking terms nor really friendly with one another we went through the usual routine of asking for I.D and eventually I made my way past him inside. I put my I.D away but in truth I might as well of kept it in my hand because believing that there's a chance of me having sneaked past the guard outside I was once more asked to present it at the bar. Once I'd past the test for a second time I found a corner and sofa of the pub to make my way towards. Unlike the pub that I, Sean, Paul and Julian had gone to this wasn't the kind of place that you could find a sofa to rest against and relax. A little bit more upbeat than what I was used to with people from a different city I was adapting to my new surroundings fast. With the lights flashing and music beating loudly I kept a mental note of the location of everyone in my head because sitting on the edge of my seat I was convinced that something might happen any one of them at any given time. It never but I felt better and more comfortable for doing so.

Inside and doing whatever I was doing more of The Leisurebox crew arrived in their droves to join us in the party. With the night going on into the long hours what happened next is beyond me and the next day another long commute looking rough as is humanly possible back home was on the cards.

I can't be sure if it was on this occasion but I do recall that one time when stood in the kitchen of the house waiting for the pizza to cook in the oven Elijah was so out of it he sat on the washer that was located behind the door that led into the kitchen, the door opened backwards so that it came into contact with the face of the washer. Jamz set the trap of leaving the door open so that if Elijah moved he'd come into contact with it but wasn't going to cause him any harm in his state of existing but sleeping on the spot. Once Elijah come to and moved he smashed his head of the edge of the door and woke up in an instant. Everyone but poor Elijah knew what had gone on and we all broke out in stitches much to his confusion.

The first visit to the pub was not the last and there'd be many more to come but all involved alcohol so not only are memories forgotten but also miss-merged with one another in terms of dates. Everyone had a good time nonetheless.

CHAPTER THIRTEEN

I've mentioned that consuming alcohol used to (I say used to because I no longer drink alcohol for this and other reasons) leave me with a red face. A drop or several bottles made none the difference since the first would transform me into a tomato and that was that. Chilli con carne it turns out did the same thing as I was about to find out the hard way.

Well, for clarification, chilli con carne never gave me alcohol flushes but rather made my face go red. Redder than alcohol as it turns out. I'd never known for me to have an actual reaction to eating something before but this would be the first and last time, thus far, I'd be tempted to try the meal.

On the menu in the cafe was new food pots that you put in the microwave for a few minutes and served up and cost about £2-3. Over the odds in price but I had suffered with spots, bad skin and a red face for so long during my youth and still did that I wanted to try something new. I should have just gone around the corner to The Dragon Inn and while it wouldn't have done my skin any good to eat from there it certainly wouldn't have given me the instant reaction that I was about to encounter. After asking Iqbal to put one in the microwave for me it was served up and I consumed it, most likely in the cupboard away from the prying eyes of customers, and thought nothing of it until I returned to the cafe for Iqbal to tell me that my face had gone bright red. A cause for concern since I'd expressed many times before to Iqbal just how conscious I was about my bad skin and I knew that he wouldn't mention it if it wasn't anything like all the other times. After telling me once and then again he asked if I was ok. I couldn't understand what the fuss was about but after a quick trip to the bathroom to check my reflection my skin was literally on fire. A quick trip to the office and I dialled 101 to ask for advice. I recall the most grim aspect of the phone call was when I had to inform them that it felt like something under my skin was moving around and irritating me. Once I'd spoken this line Karen (yes that Karen) pulled a face of disagreement and I think I'd pinpoint this memory as the one as to when I gained the opinion that she had the mental age of a child. After the phone call was over Andy, a manager, agreed to come with me to the local Boots so that I could visit the walk in centre. Upon reflection he probably only did so that I couldn't sue the company should anything of actually happened to me but at the time it seemed like a nice out of the blue gesture that I appreciated. We made our way to boots with small talk and me doing nothing but keeping my face to the ground attempting to hide my face form anyone else with an if I cannot see you then you cannot see me mentality. When we arrived the form was filled out we waited and eventually got called up and sat down around a corner and had my blood pressure taken. All in all it turned out nothing was wrong and my visit was over. I think the redness went down with time, for that day at least. Upon reflection it could have been the chilli. I mean the skin on my face is red most of the time because when I was younger I had acne and therefore used to burst loads of spots so the doctor said it could be skin damage and permanent at that and I assume combining that with casual redness of a hot chilli for someone who's not used to them turned me into a human tomato. I'd be concerned, I imagine, if I was someone else and someone else was me. I never did confirm what it was exactly since chilli con carne contains lots of different things but I ruled all of them out of my diet so I never had to find out the hard way again.

I do wonder if amongst all this Karen managed to find the time to steal the money the hockey group paid that Wednesday. In summary BCU – Birmingham City University – or a group from came to visit for an hour every Wednesday and paid good money to hire the ice so that they could practice in their numbers ice hockey. Each week it's assumed after they paid Karen would take the money and not put it in the safe as she should have done. She got caught out eventually when one Wednesday they asked for a receipt at reception and they knew nothing about it and it went from there and of course the long winded task of finding out if it was Karen on the fiddle became clear and she was gone not long after.

Oh, that's why it doesn't make sense. Colin must have still been a figure skating coach when I'd asked him about the job. In two chapters time I can say he was the rink manager for sure.

CHAPTER FOURTEEN

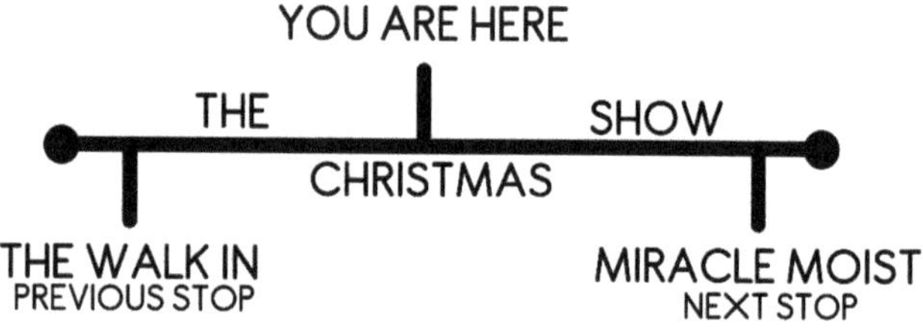

If you wish to play along at home and watch how what I'm about to describe actually happened, not that I'm telling a lie but for visual reference, then open your web browser and make your way to Youtube and perform a search for The Leisurebox. At the time of writing this the first four videos have Christmas show in their title and those would be the ones you'll need to watch.

Christmas 2013.

I'd been around since early 2012 but I hadn't ever heard talk of a Christmas show before. I recall this as my first Christmas at The Leisurebox because I don't recall a thing about Christmas 2012. I'm going to guess that at that point in time I was a steward but hadn't known anyone long enough to really make anything of it. By Christmas 2013 I'd been around an age and it was a year to celebrate. The days are numbered and fast running out however and sadly, of course unknown to me at the time, there wouldn't be another one after this.

The show was a ticketed only event. A fair but unusual event given that staff mostly got the right of god in all areas and did what they pleased regardless of what was taking place, within reason. I think Karen made this event the difference and wasn't afraid to tell the security to keep the riff raff, anyone whom hadn't paid, out. Staff, regulars, whomever. Rules are rules and all that jazz.

All the people performing in the show beside the Birmingham Ice Freestylers where figure skaters. It was us and them. Figure skaters and everyone else. Well, that's how I viewed it anyway. Fancy costumes, posh cars and an attitude like they owned the place I never really gelled nor wanted to with most of them. To me they were temporary inconveniences and to them I, and the workers, where probably the small people. I said hello to a few of the coaches and small talked here and there but on the whole I stayed well away. Colin must have been the exception to the group given he'd soon, after this event, become rink manager. No surprise then that I seem to recall not a single one of them putting in any manual graft at all towards the building of the: set, setting of out the seats, construction of the towers, spotlights etc and instead come after we'd all put the work in and gone after the show had finished. "Oh yes dear one is amused. Oh Cuthbert very well done my little darling for doing your shitty little spin on the spot" was something similar to what I was probably thinking at the time watching them doing their thing.

Despite it being a ticketed event what was the only thing that I did not do? Buy a ticket. I'd been there for so long I had it set within me that I'd somehow sneak upstairs and enjoy the show without having to shell out a single penny. Neither I nor any of the staff paid for much out the place and took more than we put into. I think I was the only person that actually paid to skate when Colin introduced a ban for the staff skating for free that once. That's a different story altogether.

I managed somehow to get upstairs and found Karen slumped in a plastic chair located near the middle entrance point located by Wendy's skate shop. A prime time for Wendy I'd imagine in the hope of attracting customers given the, all the performers, used the area from the edge of Wendy's shop to the bottom of the ice rink to get ready, dressed, warmed up and all the rest of it so had to walk past to get beyond the curtain. I've no idea why they needed such a big area given all Kevin ever said when we used the excuse that we'd need to warm up was "You're not a bloody car." Figure skaters always did over the top jumps, running up and down and all the rest of it. Give it a rest.

Sean and Kassum controlled the spotlights located on top of two constructed towers that we had to have an external company come in to construct. Kassum worked at the rink also although there's really nothing significant to say about him yet. Next chapter I'll introduce him properly.

With the plastic chairs set in place on wood that was set out on the ice so that none of the customers could make an insurance claim if they fell over trying to make their way to their seats because they weren't used to walking on ice in their shoes, unlike the staff, the show began.

Nothing significant sticks out about and my mind wonders into the direction that it would have made for a nice photograph in black and white of the people on the ice and the performers in the background. I'd not yet discovered photography and again, like many times before, had failed to appreciate the moment while I was in it so sadly, from me at least, no photographs exist of this day.

Show over with everyone made their way towards the exit and not many volunteered to help with the deconstruction of everything. I think Kevin and Paul were annoyed that none of the staff had wanted to help but I recall it being late and rather than leaving it until the next day, besides the important parts like scaffolding, they wanted it all took down and carried down the ramp there and then. I think I stayed behind but cannot be sure. Carl, the DJ, and me as I remember it. Fuzziness again.

CHAPTER FIFTEEN

11th April 2014.

We've skipped a fair bit but in truth since Christmas nothing really happened. Four months of bland nothingness and regular routine. Colin replaced Karen as rink manager and possibly Karen Yates, the cleaner, left, or was that way before? Karen's, the cleaner, departure left Rory as the sole cleaner for the entire building. Big J had punched a hole in the wall and survived his job despite Kevin's gunning for his neck and the hole had been filled despite much drama over how much it would cost. The bar had gained TV's and a darts board. I'm really just setting the scene for the final push given that it all dries up and soon, much like Zenos did, all goes downhill.

Upset in our little clouded reality aside, temporarily, it had been quite some time since I had attended a foam party. The first foam party, and the only one before this, that I'd attended occurred when I knew no one quite some time ago. Luke defiantly didn't come but I've no date so can't pinpoint it. I stood outside in the queue waiting to be let in and made friends with this lad of a similar age that latter turned up when I was either a steward of staff member and we caught up briefly but in truth it was only small talk to pass the time. I and Kassum reached the agreed conclusion, of which was made on the April 2014's foam party, that the last one had been a complete failure with a machine that spat out very little foam and only filled a small area near the corner of the rink that it was located in. I'm not sure what company they used this time around but I'd certainly hope it wasn't the same as the last. Foam party's didn't come around often and so naturally you made the most of them. I recall that on the first one Matt and Josh had got onto the ice and where given the task of shovelling the foam around all over the customers to get them into the swing of things although I don't really recall much dramas beside my Bauer Vapour TI's, yes it's that long ago, being soaked through along with my jeans. Another old mans tip of mine to the young ones is if you ever are to attend an ice rink foam party wear old clothes for the sake of preventing damaging your best ones, it's not a fashion parade.

Second, this, time around I didn't really enjoy it in the same way that I had wanted to enjoy the first. First time I wanted to skate and be out amongst the foam and enjoy it all but being a little older and having been around for a while I wanted to enjoy the day with the people that I knew and watching everyone else have fun. Don't get me wrong I still skated because I wouldn't have missed this once a year, at most, event for anything but I certainly wasn't as thrilled as previously.

A memory I cannot shake is the work of Kassum. I said I'll introduce him but there's not really a great deal to say. He liked hockey and could out skate, in terms of speed and ability, just about everyone that turned up at the place although he rarely did beside when he'd had a drink because it just didn't float his boat. He liked to work and go home at the end of it rather than hang around, in his words, with the rink rats. Rink rats being people of whom do nothing but live at the ice rink. His personality was that of someone whom like to play practical jokes and pass insults, mostly to me, a lot of the time. Classic one liners that even when I wasn't asking for it would shoot me down and I'd have nothing to come back with. You could confide in Kassum but be sure there'd be a friendly joke about it once it had all blown over, if it was a serious story for example. He was, for a long time, famous for never shaving and as a result had hair beyond what words could describe. One day he turned up with no facial hair, having at long last shaved it all off, and as a result turned up looking at least twenty years younger. He left one shift a man and returned a fresh face boy another. No one recognized him and when they did it took a while for them to accept the sight of which was in front of them. I'm sure he probably didn't hear the end of it for at least a period spanning a week.

This memory in particular was what would become the latter famous saying "More foam more moisture." A photograph uploaded on social media of a bottle of lotion with the caption "Watch out ladies Nathan Denny's on the prowl tonight" uploaded not long before the doors where open to the public. Alongside this I left my phone in skate hire on charge only to return to find quite a few selfies of Kassum and Carl, Yates not the DJ, on my phone. One small encounter that pinpoints another dot on the timeline of jokes played by Kassum at my expense. I dare to say I could write a full length book including all the ones he every performed at my expense and still manage to miss one or two. Still, at least it was a rest from the usual highlighted fact that I'd been single for a long time and at least for this point in time, of which was rare, he'd allowed me to forget it. Well, the only other one was that he also liked to point out that I had no chin and would shout at random times "No chin bitch" and alike. There was a video around at the time with the saying "No nipple bitch" on Facebook so I think that's where it came from. Upon reflection I'm not mad for the countless hours of abuse I suffered and spent on the phone to the ginger helpline because ultimately the jokes where down the fact that Kassum's home made drive by sandwich shop didn't really attract many customers at all. Hey, buddy? If you liked it then you should've put a ring on it ♪

CHAPTER SIXTEEN

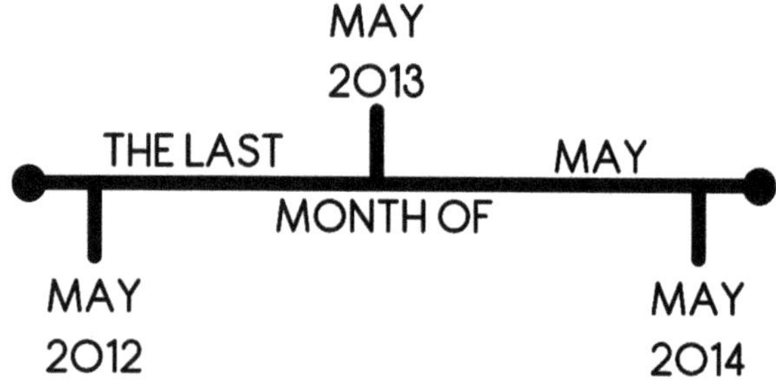

This is where the downfall begins. I'd say the main part of the main narrative comes to a sudden end and the material of what I can tell you runs thin. Beyond this the end is near.

May 2014.

We'd had a good run I and The Leisurebox but May of the aforementioned year would be the last month that the building that had stood on

Pershore Street in Birmingham since Est 1965 (source: Birmingham Mail's article No. 8499414) would be operational and beyond that would be resided to dust never to exist. The reason I ever started this manuscript beyond the Sashi episode was that I felt it important for future generations to acknowledge a piece of the history of Birmingham that once stood in a place they may pass every single day and be none the wiser. I feel lucky to have discovered it and been a part of what it was but I can't help but feel that the building should have been grade listed and protected from demolition even if the rink would have shut and some other business come along I wouldn't have minded versus the plan that was soon announced that it would be turned into flats. Then again I suppose if plans can be put forward for the base that Winston Churchill used to win World War Two to be turned into flats, luxury apartments or alike (source: Daily Mail's article No. 3874894) then it's understandable that we stood no chance. I'm not bitter because I've long moved on but what a thing to discover, live through and then end. I'd live it all again if I could. I can't say I'd work at an ice rink again because I've had my time and it's well and truly in the past. I tried to apply at Blue Ice Solihull after we'd closed when I heard Kassum might be getting a shot at a job down there but nothing come of it. I wasn't in the click and I don't think they'd extend an arm of help even if they had a position. I know a few decent folk from the place but I don't think much of it for the most part and even less now than Planet Ice have purchased it and taken over. I'd hazard a guess that one day one of them might be penning a story about their time. The right decision in the long run for I don't think it's much of a career. Letting go took a while but what can you do when there's nothing to hold on to?

I'll continue this closer to the end.

CHAPTER SEVENTEEN

One of the last adventures that I'm glad, in the grand scheme of things, that I discovered just shy of The Leisurebox closing was photography. I ordered a Nikon D5200 from eBay, of all places, some months before May 2014 and as a result spent the summer investing every bit of spare time and money into it. Paul and Kevin, as it turns out, had a great passion for photography also and eventually we'd discover so would Lee, another manager, and the four of us spent many hours standing at the bowling desk discussing nothing but. Kevin used to do adult shoots and develop the photographs afterwards and shot all sorts. He came into work with some photographs that you had to hold up to the light to see and upon reflection I didn't really appreciate this as much as I should have. What a gem to own. Shame I've since lost contact with Kevin.

On the other side of the coin photography is a double edged sword because while I discovered it at The Leisurebox and loved it for so long the closure of the rink has affected my want to shoot, so to speak, ever since we closed. I've shot a few locations but have been out maybe only a handful of days at the very most in the two years since. I've since purchased a Tamron 70-300mm and a Tamron 24-70mm, in that order, but even they are just valuable assets crying to be used. Oh, and the 24-70mm I purchased brand new from Jessops for almost £800, I must have been mad. A life changing amount of money I'd forgotten about until writing this in truth.

To revert the timeline to what I should be talking about all I had at this point in time, in terms of photography kit, beside the camera was a Nikon 18-55mm that came with the camera and a Nikon 50mm prime. Good enough for amateur street photography but not really nearly enough for what was about to come next. Natalie, the same Natalie of whom had interviewed me for the job I'd now been working in for almost a year, asked me to be the photographer at her baby's christening. It's a big thing to get your first proper gig as a photographer and each customer is highly valued so naturally I did my best to ensure that Natalie fully understood that I wasn't anything more than an amateur. I shot: buildings, stationary cars, street lamps, alley ways and so on not special events. I probably sold myself short and gave her more than enough room to say "No, ok then, that's fine" but she never did and that was that. I was doing it whether I felt confident or not.

When the day of the shoot arrived the anxiety kicked in and again I was out of my comfort zone. It turns out that the church was located quite close to my house but of course I wasn't aware and so wanting to set a good impression I phoned for a taxi hours before the time I'd been given as the start. The only line I recall the taxi driver saying was "What part of the Warwick Road mate it's quite long?" and then suddenly we'd arrived. I spent what seemed like forever standing at the roadside guarding my bag full of photography gear like a pit-bull at the church entrance and eventually plucked up the courage to walk onto the church grounds. On my way walking slowly I recall a couple passing me and telling me to go in, I didn't, and lingered outside some more. When I'd eventually had enough of all the waiting I walked inside like a lost stranger and quietly, like an invisible ghost, made my way past all the people inside to the back row of the seating and started fumbling around with my camera bag. I unpacked and checked everything as many times as was humanly possible but in truth all I was doing was blocking out my surroundings and finding comfort in something that I was used to. The idea of all these new people around me was terrifying and the last thing I wanted was to catch the eye of any one of them and start a conversation. I recall praying that any moment now that familiar faces would rush through the doors and take their seats ready for the event. Before they did I managed to catch the eye of one person, the vicar, and we had a chat about why I was here "I'm the photographer" I introduced myself and we had a chat about what was and what wasn't allowed. I had enough common sense to respect the fact that he wasn't telling me yes and no to set questions for the fun of it and much rather I had to listen, if I liked it or not, to what he wanted. Flash wasn't allowed and nor was standing at the front of the church where they perform the actual christening. I was most annoyed about the latter part of that list of do nots because I'd planned to get some close ups and didn't really have the kit to zoom in on the baby's face and reaction as the water was placed on the forehead. I missed some valuable shots because of this but rules are rules. The chat with the vicar had led me to near the front row of the seating and after not very long at all I turned around to notice people arriving. I was grateful because we could finally start counting down the clock of how soon this would all be over and I could find myself, once more, back on familiar ground but at the same time my anxiety couldn't stop telling me that one of them was going to steal some part of my gear that I'd left sprawled out on the back row so I broke the conversation with the vicar of and made my way back to the gear.

When the christening started I was ready but I wasn't. I was in the room physically but mentally I was elsewhere. The lights where on but no one was home. I'd spent my time before everyone else arrived standing around and talking to the vicar and now, when it mattered, I had photographs to take but didn't know the first thing about what settings to use. The church looked bright enough inside to the naked eye but on the camera it all came out, as I'd expected, differently. I spent the first part of the shoot hiding behind a pillar to the right of the church out of sight of everyone while I got the settings and what lens to use right. After I'd got that down and finished faffing around I came out and made my way to the back of the isle behind the last person in the last row so that I wasn't blocking anyone's view. I caught the eye of Rob, the same Rob as all that time ago that opened the doors on our first visit, as we nodded at one another to say hi as we hadn't much chance beforehand and continued with what I was doing. All I was really doing in truth was taking a photograph and checking it for dark spots, noise, shadows and so on. I took as many as possible so that I had a lot to work with back home. With street photography you can just re-visit the location and re-shoot but on a day and one of event like this I had to make the most of it while I was there so that post shoot photographs came out as good as possible. Keeper images where gold dust on days like this and I wanted as many as possible.

After the event was over the final task in the church was to take photographs of groups of people standing by the alter. Natalie and Danny, her partner, stood at the alter and decided who they wanted photographs with and I gave the nod when I was done. In truth I should have spoken up a bit more because the world and his wife with their phones surrounded me and started taking pictures of their own. I always remember feeling regret, afterwards, that I didn't take charge and tell them all to look into the camera and so on. A real photographer would have probably walked out when people started taking snaps on their phone blocking their view and line of image but I didn't really feel like I could do anything. I managed to get some keeper images but I had to put some on the final DVD that I had no option but to otherwise it would have looked like certain people hadn't attended at all.

We then made our way outside and I took a lift with Manish, Lee and, I believe, Paul. Manish being the driver. I hadn't arranged a lift as I'm not entirely sure that I was aware there was an after party. I recall standing outside and awkwardly standing around with my thumb out and a sign around my neck like "Any takers?" Naturally Manish was more than willing but I didn't exactly plan it well.

When we arrived I found myself, again, in a room full of people that I do not know. The people from the church plus more, I think. The anxiety struck again and I told Natalie that I'd let everyone arrive and settle down before I started with the photographs. In truth I was shitting bricks and didn't have the confidence to walk up to someone like "You alright mate, can I have a photo of your face please?" When you live with something like anxiety you learn the coping mechanisms that prevent everyone else from constantly asking "You alright?" and thinking that you're anything but normal. I sat at a table with people that I knew and was given a gentle nudge by Lee after a while with something along the lines of "When are you going to start the photos?" I'd been sitting at the table and relaxing for so long I'd forgotten why I was there. Natalie wasn't against me enjoying myself since I'm sure the invite was extended to the after party if I was photographing or not but I wasn't being paid to sit around so I think Lee said what she didn't want to. I'm not saying Natalie ever gave me that impression but I'm sure she would have at some point if Lee didn't. Being allowed to withdraw into a dark corner I'd have hidden away and pretended I wasn't the photographer if I could have.

I walked around the room after fumbling around in my photography bag fixing a lens to the camera and approached the first person that I was to take a picture of. I remember her always because after I'd done everyone's photographs I sat back down and viewed through them only to find that the first two, of this female, had become so dark and the settings where so wrong that I knew there was no saving them even if I lifted the shadows and performed some magic they'd still be second rate. The trick is to get it as close to perfect on the camera as possible and then you can make the small adjustments on the computer. You can get it wrong in camera and recover it afterwards but an almost black image is beyond saving. The fault could have been the camera still being on the settings that suited the church but in truth the room was dark in places and most likely the limiting F stop on the lenses probably weren't allowing enough light in to capture a good image. Problem was if you put the ISO up you get more noise and if you slow down the shutter speed to let more light in you get blurry images. In the grand scheme of things you'll be glad to know after plucking up the courage to ask for a second image, in fear of sounding like a weirdo, I got the shot I needed and she found herself on the list of keeper images on the final DVD.

After the photographs of everyone I took some shots of the food and the kids dancing but beyond that I resided to the table I sat at. Stephanie, Davie, Manish, Lee, Paul and Davie's wife. A family get together in a way given all beside Davie's wife had, at some point, worked at The Leisurebox. Stephanie had left The Leisurebox, as an employee, before I'd arrived on the scene but I got to know better as time went on and as she re-visited on social events like this. Not entirely friendly as in we'd go for a drink down the pub but we'd say hi if we came across one another. Small talk and alike. Davie was the same, left before I'd got there, but I'd encountered him in my Steward days as I recall him walking in once in a meeting that we were having in the bar. "It may be a shit hole but it's our shit hole" and it stuck with me ever since. Plus it was nice to see Manish again. I'm not sure that I've seen him since in truth. Well, then again I've not seen anyone for a long time.

Raffina, Shiv and Natalie turned up latter than everyone else. Girls from work. Raffina had an interest in photography so I allowed her to look through the raw files on the camera of what I'd taken. I took some more of Raffina and the girls and then put the camera away for the last time. Carl and his wife also attended with his two kids. I remember one of them being called Nathan but I forget the girls name. Carl, not to be confused with Carl the DJ or steward, was a tall chap that attended the ice rink with his wife and kids once a week, usually on weekends, and got on really well with a lot of people. Type of family that really leave a good impression on you and you look back on in later life thinking "I'm glad that we crossed paths if only for a little while." I used to receive texts from Carl every Friday asking for skate 120_ to be sharpened, about the only time I ever made use of my qualification, and then latter on he'd turn up, I'd hand them over to him and we'd all be happy. Always complemented the cut I gave the blades and said he wouldn't skate without a fresh pair because it made all the difference. He was telling the truth but I'm not sure I was really that good at sharpening them more like the only one, beside Big J, that ever touched the machine and did some real work on the blades.

I departed, eventually, and returned to The Leisurebox where outside I met Sean, Iqbal and a few others. Of course I still had my suit on and carrying all my gear so the lads made some comments like "You've gone all out" and "Look at you" given that it was a rare occasion that they'd seen me dressed up. Probably a photograph or two floating around on Instagram of me in such attire.

I almost started to edit the photographs in the pub given that I had my laptop, for whatever reason, with me but it was painfully slow and would have been rude and unfair on the others. My monitor at home provides far better results so it was probably the better decision in truth.

The alcohol took over and memory fades.

The last Sunday before The Leisurebox closed. The first time we, as a group, had all gotten together and enjoyed a social event in for as long as I could remember. In less than forty eight hours on from this moment in time it would all, for the last time, come to an abrupt end.

If anything I'm glad that we all had one last weekend together because it was almost like an inadvertent parting. Even if I did wish afterwards (once we'd all been made redundant) that I should had saved all the money I'd just spent the weekend before I now think that the memories last far longer than the money ever could have so don't regret a single part of it. We visited Dudley that weekend to attend Steph's birthday party but ended up at JB's pub after not very long at all. Sean stayed at mine, again, and all was well in the world.

Things seemed on the up. How very wrong I was indeed.

CHAPTER EIGHTEEN

The Last Time

Was The Leisurebox a drug? Was it my drug? Was I addicted?

Like those questions and many more they can never be answered. Like my former self The Leisurebox, that provides all the answers, is long gone. It's a strange one because it's something that I realised from the start and yet in the end would be the creating of my downfall. My realisation was that all that time ago with Luke when there was so many happy hours ahead of me I never, ever, wanted to miss not a single hour. Throughout my entire time this remained with me and if ever I did then I had a feeling in my gut, an unbearable one, that I was missing something. Home was The Leisurebox and every time someone wanted to spend even a minute away from it I'd find that it wasn't far away from the front of my mind.

Sunday was Natalie's christening but Monday was just another day. I had photographs to edit sure but she hadn't set a timeline and Monday was hockey day with the lads. So very long ago I'd tried ice hockey, like actually taken part, but found that a few people that took part I didn't really like and therefore didn't want them to bash me up against a barrier with more intent than the instructor, Paul, was telling them to. I gave up, regrettably, after not very long at all. Back when I did it there was Paul and another chap. I don't recall much other than he sure made an impression on me. I just always remember him is all. For so long, since I'd got my Nikon, I'd re-found the passion of ice hockey but instead had taken to photographing it rather than taking part. At first I flashed my camera around like I was the best thing in the world. On the first day I followed Kassum, Aron and Jamz to the local empty car park down Pershore Street, not NCP but the bigger one next to it, and took shots of the car park, hockey sticks, them and everything. I remember two guys standing around the corner with beer in their hands and never returned to the car park after that. On my own I'm sure they'd have tried something but four guys and a few hockey sticks I escaped with my camera. I don't mean they tried anything on but it was a little naive of me to venture into that side of town flashing around hundreds of pounds worth of goods just dangling from my hands. Everyone likes photography but the one thing on the mind constantly is which one of these people looking at my camera is going to attempt to snatch it out of my hand and make a run for it? Street photography is rewarding but at times you find yourself wondering the streets alone in places you question what might happen if you weren't there on that day in that time frame. I did a walk of town recently by the old Birmingham Library, the one that's just been demolished (2016. Designed by John Madin and was located in Chamberlain Square), and because of the construction zone I was re-directed down an alley way and was asking myself the same question, who's going to come either end of this alley and rob me? I made it out but like the shots you take you have to pick your moments to get the camera out. Birmingham's not all that bad but there's an art to it all. Anyway, this Monday was different because before leaving the house for once I wasn't tempted to grab my camera and instead after much repetitive "Just do it" by Kassum I'd decided that for the first time in a long time I was going to re-join the group rather than continue to take the same images week in week out. I got three quarters of the way down my road when my phone buzzed, a text from Aaron, and he reminded me that today, this Monday, was a bank holiday and therefore Paul had cancelled the session. No bother, I thought, and placed the phone in my pocket and walked back home. There's always tomorrow I foolishly thought. What I hadn't known is that Sean and others had visited the rink on that day but for whatever reason it had skipped my mind to turn up, like many times before, and randomly bump into people.

The last time that walking down the road with ice skates in my hand would be considered, by me, normal. I always carried hockey protectors, like socks but in the same shape as the blade, over my skates but you still got funny looks. The looks weren't from cops but people on the bus, passers-by and so on. I used to like standing on the bus with ice skates exposed in my hand because it was a symbol. Some people didn't even now the place had reopened since it shut so that goes to show how much Birmingham knew about what was going on under its nose.

The last time. The last time the building would be operational. The last time I'd get to skate. The list goes on but the fact remains it was the last time, for the most part, for everything.

This, for others, is where the memoir would end however I consider myself lucky that I got to experience what comes next and able to provide an additional two chapters because of it.

Three hundred and sixty five days had become forty eight hours and, at long last, the day had finally arrived.

CHAPTER NINETEEN

Tuesday May 6th 2014.

Turns out it was a little longer than three hundred and sixty five days after all.

I awoke in the morning and the day started like any other. I opened my phone and checked various social media apps like always. The only difference would be that today when I opened Facebook I wouldn't exactly be greeted with joy for the world, my entire world, would come crashing down in an instant and The Leisurebox episode of my life would be over in a flash.

The first message that I came across was from Steph, Steph whom I'd started working with just over a year ago, and was something to the effect of "Has anyone got any jobs going? Just been sacked." Scrolling down and not thinking nothing of it I then came across a similar message from Lee "Just been made redundant." In truth I couldn't take it all in and had no idea what was going on. I hadn't heard any news and when I first read Steph's message I honestly thought that she'd been sacked but then Lee's message confused that theory. More and more messages I recall scrolling past but why have all these people been told and I was none the wiser? Am I the only one left? What's going on? I had no text from any of my managers and no prior warning at all. I awoke that morning and found out on Facebook. Well, I hadn't really yet found out anything because I was still in a state of denying the obvious in front of me. I'd ask you to understand my confusion given everything had been ok for years and then suddenly without warning there's signs of it all ending in a flash.

I got up, dressed and then took the bus to town. I arrived at the rink and the lights in reception where still on but no one was inside. The building was in a state of operation but no one was around.

It was like I'd walked in moments after a bomb had gone off and wiped everyone out but the furniture remained, for now, intact. I come across no one downstairs so made my way to skate hire where I found Big J. He was wearing company uniform and ready to serve customers only more relaxed than normal. He, the poor sod, had turned up for work as usual only to get part way through the shift to then be called to a meeting held in the cafe area and told that it was over. I envy that at least they were told. I assume Colin called a meeting and sent them home but for whatever reason he'd gone back upstairs and stayed. Maybe I'd caught him in-between being told and leaving.

When I eventually did come across the managers none of them had an answer. Everything was unfolding and no one had any idea what was going on. Paul came upstairs and told us all to leave and that was to be it. I took a few photographs because I didn't know if I'd ever see it again and then made my way downstairs and outside.

I stood around outside and chatted with a few others for good reason. I'd spotted a gap in the market and wanted to make myself a few extra pounds. I went inside and Kevin approached me at reception. He asked if I wanted to help out during the following weeks to empty the place and I nodded, in sign of acceptance, while thanking him and then made my way outside. In an instant it was all over but at least thanks to Kevin I'd now not only have a chance to say goodbye to the place but to make myself some extra money in the process.

While lingering around outside the disabled group that turned up from time to time arrived ready for their regular visit but as they approached we had to give them the, to us, bad news:

Us - "It's closed, sorry mate."
Them - "Oh, how come?"
Us - "It's shut down, today, it's closed for good."
Them - "When was this decision made?"

I always found that question striking. Just exactly when was this decision made? Who knew and who didn't? I'd awoken not long before and made my way here because I wanted to find out what was going on but in truth I had no idea if everyone that worked there knew or not. Some people we worked with came and went as they pleased as they had university and other jobs on the go. Our contracts where zero hours and therefore literally once you'd gotten a job it was set in stone because all you had to do was turn up one day and ask for a couple of shifts here and there and you'd be back in the clique. Floaters I referred to them as. The truth was that as time went on during the final weeks suspicion arose that some people within the company new months before and said nothing but I at the very least never did get confirmation.

Us - "This morning."

The reply to the above question and very possibly a lie. It was our truth but was it really the truth?

Them - "Oh, ok."

After that he turned to his fellow work mate and started talking about where else was open that they could go. He didn't have an ounce of emotion and instead said it like it was nothing. I've no idea if they tried to return but I never saw them after this. The group always stuck out because one guy amongst them had a habit of going from the bowling lane, often unnoticed, and to the toilet quite a few times. We, the staff, never had any idea what he was up to, if anything, but it's just how I remember them. That and the woman carer that came with them some times that was a little rough for my liking. This whole conversation and their reaction summed it up really. An event unfolding in front of very eyes that literally no one knew about because customers where still arriving like everything was normal only to find out the truth.

Before I departed Kevin and I couldn't have been more upfront and honest with one another if we tried. We'd worked together for so long that we'd had plenty of good times and now it was time to stand tall and smile to one another amongst the bad times. He'd gone from allowing me to be a steward to working with me for just over a year. We agreed the entire thing was shit but none of it was our fault and we'd done all we could to keep the building for as long as was possible and eventually, as much as we'd overlooked, one day it was going to come to an end. Sods law. No point being sad or annoyed because nothing was going to chance the decision. It was fun while it lasted. Onwards and upwards.

Approximately nineteen days before my nineteenth birthday and I was being made redundant. A sad truth of what the young workforce of the modern United Kingdom have to face. At eighteen years old I'd left a job, had been sacked from a job and been made redundant, what a trip my young working life had been thus far.

The way I remember that day is not all of what I've just written but much rather I like to look at and day dream to the photograph that I took of the sky that day. I took it on my iPhone and in truth couldn't hold more value if it tried. Standing outside I pointed the camera up and took an image that managed to capture the front of the buildings big banner with the blue sky and white clouds in the background with a bird, I forget what type, flying over and all of this captured in a moment lasting forever. A clear, almost, blue sky day with the sun shining.

"Be free my bird and on to the next adventure."

CHAPTER TWENTY

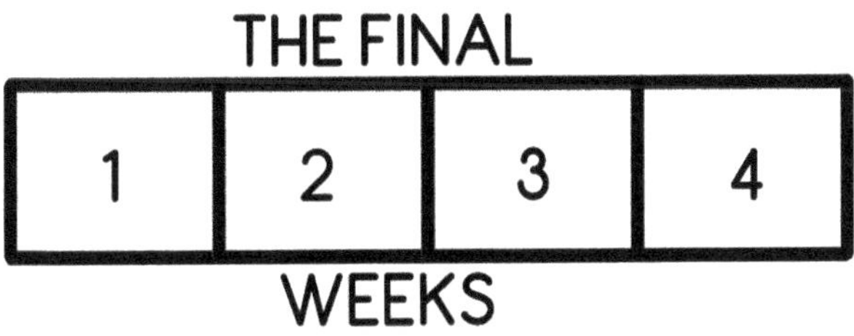

The final four weeks of my journey at The Leisurebox had, in an instant, sadly arrived. Four weeks sounds like an awfully long time when I sit here and write about it because to contemplate how much you can get done in four weeks I come to the conclusion that, given some planning, one could achieve quite a large amount. I consider that the hitch during the final four weeks at The Leisurebox was that while we had a task in hand, the sole reason we kept on after closure, what I really wanted to do was to fall flat on my face and capture things as they were in an instant and thus never having to say goodbye to them. The work allowed me to say goodbye to the place in my own way but I didn't, sadly, get to do half of what I wanted to get done during those four weeks. I however managed to find some solace during lunch times and tea breaks in taking in the small details that presented themselves in front of me while the others gathered on the bowling lanes and around the cafe area thus allowing me to, once my final goodbye had been said, to take the memory and location with me in later life. Most importantly being that that latter life would represent a future time whereby, yet to happen, The Leisurebox would not exist in physical terms. I studied the details that seemed important to me throughout those four weeks to ensure that the memory was preserved. The message I wanted to take forward was here was a building that, as I understand it, had stood since the 1960's and yet all future generations would know of it was perhaps a whisper or two from their parents in years to come of how once upon a time they enjoyed many a late night on the weekend in an environment that they had nothing to show for it beside perhaps a picture or two. In my wondering state amongst my colleagues filling their faces with food I felt it my duty to ensure that an account of all that had happened in the years leading up to the buildings final days was documented for I believe a work of literature far outlives its author and that by, at a later date, putting the memories I was observing into writing I could complete my task and thus ensure that the world, in any given time period, could look back and enjoy The Leisurebox just as much as I once had. I believed I'd finally found a way to ensure that never again in my gut would I have a feeling that I'd be missing out on something by not being at The Leisurebox because forever I could read and re-read countless times my story and with it upon each time of reading a different memory would come and go. The physical goodbye was by no means an actual goodbye for it was my start of a bigger task in hand.

To start writing about the start of the end I feel it only appropriate that first I should introduce those of whom I shared the final four weeks with: Kassum, Andy, Josh, Paul, Kevin, Iqbal, Connal, Carl Yates and Rory. The Leisurebox's very own dream team. It does somewhat leave me surprised writing that list of names just how many, some of whom dedicated many hours of their time to the building, are not amongst them. I feel this only echo's the fortune behind the position that I now found myself in.

The first day, I've no accurate date, was the best

because beyond that it turned into a second by second battle to destroy the place that for long so I'd put so much time and effort into up keeping. It was counter-productive to every fibre in my being but it had to be done. With each day that passed it was one closer to the end of the end. The first day resembled what it had been like since the first time I'd walked in but beyond that things moved faster than I'd ever imagine possible. The arcade I recall I, Sashi and Matt spending time in forever ago during a lost summer had already, not straight away but somewhere down the line, had the machines taken away and only a few remained awaiting removal. I found myself standing around in what was once a somewhat occupied arcade imagining what the rest looked like in my mind while the building was in operation because I had not yet entirely accepted that the machines, and soon everything else to follow, was and would be gone for good. The slot machines I'd won out of once or twice had been taken also. Unlike the slot machines I couldn't leave The Leisurebox while I was ahead and felt only the urge to continue. Gambling wasn't my addiction but spending as much time at The Leisurebox sure is as close as I've thus far ever come to having one.

In the midst of losing my job and somehow managing to think on my feet and land an extra four extra weeks worth of work what I hadn't taken into account was how I'd get to and from

The Leisurebox. In the past, during the NCP episode, I had learnt just how to and what it meant to hold on to every penny I owned because I wasn't sure where the next bit of income would come from. After my bus pass, if I owned one, ran out I decided that a daysaver, costing £3.90 at the time (now costs £4.60 two years on), was too much expense and instead would get the red mountain bike that had resided in my back garden and use it as my main mode of transport. Further cutbacks in the forms of food and drink where to be urgently made. I decided that the luxury of popping into the local shops, like I'd done for an age, for some lunch wasn't an option and therefore decided to live on what was available for free. In the cafe area the drinks machine remained hooked up to the partly used boxes of Fanta, Coke etc that had been hooked up just before we closed. The nacho's in the machine, likewise, where left to rot. Burgers, chips, hotdogs and whatever else was stored in the freezer had been taken out before we got a chance to enjoy our last Iqy burger, a burger that contained whatever combination you required providing it was cooked on the hush hush and eaten out the back. I made use of both the remaining fluid and nacho's in my bid to save money from the start. The drinks ran out before the nacho's and by the time I'd finish with them they'd become hard and probably tasted beyond description but I wolfed them down regardless.

Filling a cup up at a time, because the cups had been left behind, I probably took a good two to three weeks to finish whatever was left behind. I don't recall, not surprisingly, anyone else being keen on adopting my money saving method. I took visits with the others to the local chip shop, dixy and so on but never purchased anything because I was in my zone of financial doom and gloom. Even things like the one pound phone sim card that Iqbal purchased for me after I wanted to change my number in an attempt to remove the Sashi episode, still ongoing at the time, from my life was paid back the next day in full because despite him saying "Don't worry about it" I knew that answer was the one of the Iqbal before we closed for good speaking rather than the truth of what was ahead of us. I'd imagine that spending ceased at The Dragon Inn also but we had a few sessions, somewhat, after we'd been made redundant but just not as luxurious as many times before. In the past it had been plate after plate of scampi and chips "That all be me please" and bottle after bottle of Kopparberg but now was more like a Coke and maybe one beer. Iqbal was generous, in the past, with how many drinks he used to buy I and Sean but I encouraged him not to bother now. I understood and respected more making my own way. Iqbal still made the effort mind as after all when my nineteenth birthday did arrive, the last one we'd spend together, he took me to Rory's pub, or his family pub, and we sat in a private back room watching the T.V, standing outside in the courtyard talking and enjoying what was left of our time together. Good old Iq. The only one, along with Rory and Iq's cousins, to turn up on gay pride weekend for my nineteenth birthday. I'll always remember and be thankful for that. "You find out who your true friends are at times like these." Very true indeed, my friend.

Being released from The Leisurebox and NCP had two things in common in that the days before I was sacked from NCP I had been given a complete set of new uniform and chose to leave them in a room at the main car park and I'd pick and choose what I needed every shift. The managers told me to take it home but I never did. When I was sacked I had a manager, Craig, as much as my skin crawls to write that name, follow me, quite literally, out of the office and to the room I kept my uniform in where he collected it up in front of me and I assume took it back to the office as I made my way off site for good. The Leisurebox relates because I'd just been given, well, not long ago, a black fleece that I'd wear when working upstairs in skate hire and had grown quite attached to it. I left it upstairs in a disused staff room that I've no idea how I discovered existed but quite liked how away from everything it was once I did. I never spent too long up there because you could lose track of time and get locked in quite easily if you did. I recall the room with more worth than it was due. In reality it contained nothing more than two, maybe three, chairs and a table. Well, those and the pizza adverts and numbers that where pinned to a notice board. The only person that ever used this room was Kassum, to keep his hockey hit in and Rory to keep his clothes, that he changed into before and after his shift, in. In the far right upper corner of the room, as if you'd just walked through the door, there was a little hatch that had pipping behind and was really dark inside. The hatch was big enough for someone to get through and into but I never liked the look of what was behind from a distance so didn't get too close. On occasion Sean and others used to hide Rory's clothes in there and he'd spend an age trying to find them. "Bastards you lot" and the signal had passed that he'd found them at long last. When I walked in the room "They've took it already" I said to myself. I'd suspected as much but hadn't quite expected it so quickly. I adapted and brought a hoodie with me after that. Colin made a big fuss about these jackets because he liked to point out, more than once and very loudly indeed, that he'd paid for them out of his own pocket whereas upon reflection he most probably got them on the cheap from the local rag market located literally around the corner. Uniform wasn't a thing at The Leisurebox because most of us ignored it. We got told of mind, when it was open, for what we wore but none of us really played an ounce of attention beyond the repetitive and formal sounding responded of "Sorry and I won't do it again."

With the bike, my bicycle, residing in the cafe leant against a wall, the only time I'd imagine a bicycle would be allowed in the cafe, we set to work. At first it was easy jobs like turning the plant of and waiting for the ice pad to melt but since that took longer than we'd imagined, at first, we all split ways and took the small jobs instead. Most of the time, for the early part, I spent with Iqbal and we'd often make our way to Tesco for five minute walks in-between working hours. There wasn't a hard and fast rule of when you could and couldn't take a rest because the worst that could happen was you would get told to go home. It never happened mind but we'd already lost our jobs so the authority of the managers had come down a peg or two. I'd imagine that it was on one of these trips to Tesco with Iqbal that the group came along and found walking me with a little weird when they discovered I'd gone in and purchased a bag of sub one pound tortillas and started grabbing them one at a time and eating through them. I got funny looks from just about anyone who wasn't with us also but I couldn't have cared less given what had happened to our jobs. I think Kassum tagged me in a few photos on Facebook of guys standing on the street with loafs of bread afterwards. See, there's more than one of us. I made that packet last a few days and mixed up some mouldy tortillas with it. Genius.

The fourth floor would be where I spent most of my time working during these four weeks and in truth was the area of the ice rink I was most in love with. I call it the fourth floor but from ground level it was the second, located above the ice rink. I say fourth because the building had four floors in total and that count includes the often forgotten basement. The only two floors that people, customers, got to see was the ground floor and first. I liked sneaking away up to the top floor because it had so much hidden history in plain sight. I used to like watching the long since unused features like the bar and playing movies in my head of what parties must have looked like here in the past. Of course it had long been forgotten but I could, and probably did, spend hours up there away from everyone without wanting to come down. What was left of this floor was: A nightclub, cafe, gym, dance and the seating area that ran all the way around the windows that in their hay day people would have sat in to watch the ice skating. The seats however only remained at the back end of the ice rink now unlike as before when they used to run on all three sides. The nightclub had remnants of what remained form the 70's and 80's approx. The cafe was of a similar age. The gym only had two separate changing room blocks left that I'd imagine would have been male and female. I forgot about the kitchen beside the nightclub, bit oddly placed. That and the two office looking structures at the back of the kitchen that I stood in and imagined being of importance at some point in the past although now where as derelict as could get. After I first discovered this floor I used to come up all the time to take photographs and would find a new subject on every occasion. The amount of chairs, tables and wood that was around scared me because I always recall thinking that if someone wanted to shut us down for good then setting all this on fire would be a good start because the place would soon be up in flames crumbling in ashes. The upper floor was huge and open. I'd like to have seen it in its hay day but have only come across a limited number of photographs online. The salsa bar, or nightclub area, still had a few pumps attached although the barrels had long gone. The cloakroom and toilets still remained also although where so unlit it was hard to see inside. The stairs that led up to the nightclub was so badly damaged and the roof caved in that I never went down because it was as unsafe as could get and even standing on the landing looking over the banister gave me the creeps. I recall the story that a workman had died building the place although cannot recall if it related to this part of the building. Andy had shown I and Steph a hatch that led down into a dark room that the only exit was this hatch we were looking through when we first joined although despite how many times I looked for it I could never find it. We didn't dare to go inside. We've no idea why it was ever built. I recall the room at the back end, by the seats, of the upper floor because it had a blue carpet, holes in the window and a damaged roof that birds used to live in. Andy took us up there, I and someone else, in an attempt to show us this regular bird that came to and fro but we never got to see it. This room again only had one door to get in and out and was most likely some form of private office although had literally nothing inside and had long been vacated. What all this did do was create a good scene for hide and seek. I, Siraj and someone else played it on several occasions and I managed to walk in a dark unlit room and past him and out again without even noticing. Games didn't last for though given that was when we were operational and I was always cautious about who would come up stairs even though it was obvious that no one ever would. My anxiety again. A floor with no CCTV you could get away with anything. Not that I ever did anything mind unlike the stories I was told that occurred in the 1970's to do with managers and possibly attractive young looking women in hidden away offices. I'll leave it to your imagination and include no names.

Just like the upstairs had been its own separate

venue in the 1970's and 1980's another feature of the same period in time but resided one floor lower, connected to the ice rink, was the stage. The stage in the modern era meant absolutely nothing to anyone who hadn't been around at that time, or that knew what it was, because for so long it hadn't existed you'd be forgiven for not knowing and or forgetting entirely about it. I've seen images of what it looked like but it was so different during my stay even I struggled to picture how everything really was back then when it was operational. All that remained in the modern day was a small hut that was accessed via a door located in the current DJ booth that ran along the back wall of the ice rink. Like many other rooms in this building it had one way in and one way out. The corridor that ran along the back was on strict accesses terms because the pit, that always had its doors open, where on the other side. If you fell in the pit you'd be dead because it dropped all the way down the building and had slanted slopes so you couldn't help yourself up. Now that I think about it I wonder if the one time that I was in skate hire and a group of three males approached with one of them drenched in water because the one of them had just fallen into the pit had anything to do with it. To do with the rink closing that is. I was a little innocent back then but now that I think about it how the place wasn't sued I'll never now because the pit door had been left open with me on shift and Lee as the manager. Lee had gone, as far as I recall, home when Colin took over the shift as he found himself in the middle of a disaster. I won't forget the look on his face when I told him that the lad had fallen into the pit. There must have been some sugar coating and sweet talking. I recall a rumour floating around that the kid wanted £10,000 otherwise he'd go to court, or was that what he wanted via a court case? I don't recall what come of it, if anything. I'm surprised that the two lads that had gone skating with him had managed to pull him out. I don't think they knew what they had gotten themselves into otherwise there might have been a bit more panic involved. You'd only be able to understand the story if you had seen the pit in person. I don't know how many people knew about it but I doubt its something anyone raved about. I kept my job and so did Lee and I don't recall ever being involved in an investigation, an internal one, so maybe that's why the memories faded for so long. The barrier should have been shut but in truth the barrier was just a thing piece of wood that ran along the main barrier to prevent you from falling in. Held in place by two, maybe four, bolts that went into holes in the barrier it was shabby at best. The two doors that ran over the pit should have always been closed in truth but they never did. I'm lost for words about the incident in truth. I don't have a date of occurrence sadly.

Before I departed for the final time on one of the

final days I finally got an invite to see the basement. It would be the first and last time I'd be able to do so. To get to the basement you had to walk through where the arcade once stood, through a door into the workshop, through another door behind the bowling machines and then down the long alley way to turn left and then right through a singular door down some very old steps indeed. The steps where the kind you find outside like old metal emergency exit steps. Very narrow and thin in width of the staircase. Something like what reside on outer buildings of apartments in New York City. I'd love to tell you what was downstairs but all I recall was a huge, much bigger than I, Planet Ice sign that must have been down here for an age. Everything else was, room wise, was flooded. The main reason we'd been invited down, I recall now that there was three of us staff on this tour, was that when we walked around the corner two managers jumped out and gave us a scare. The two, I forget who, who I was with stayed put whereas I turned around and started running only to stop in my tracks and turn back when I realized what was going on. Paul was giving the tour and had been speaking extra loud so the managers could hear where we were for this exact reason, sod. I recall one particular room right at the back that was quite literally knee deep in water. Shame I don't have any photographs.

Before we left we were allowed to take some of the glasses from the bar but I decided against because I had no idea what they'd been through in their time and in truth most of them probably had fur in them because they never got used. Iqbal took a bin bag full if I recall correctly. I'd hope he managed to get them back home in one piece. I took four hockey pucks donated by Rory since he thought that I needed them more than he did and some CD's of music we played in a long gone by summer while consuming alcohol and playing pool.

Generosity was, at times, met with idioticness during our four week stay as the entire story had two main jokes. Firstly would be finding out via social media and secondly would be the insult of Colin standing over us telling us to leave the place spotless, as in literally get the brush and pan out, when we had finished working. We all laughed to ourselves and never acted upon it.

I realize I've skipped over the main narrative that you probably wish to read about what went where and what we did on what days and so on but the truth is beyond bubble wrapping a few items and moving boxes we spent hours literally being removal men. All I can say in the interest of keeping it simple is that everything that was inside we moved out piece by piece. By the end of it you could be forgiven for not recognizing what had once stood where. I suppose I could tell you that the container that was dropped outside, literally a shipping container, because you find them for hire all the time, was filled with: gloves, socks, backpacks, glow-sticks, pencil cases and whatever other branded items we'd sold via reception before closure. It took an absolute age to throw them all the way down from the top floor to street level. I've no idea where the container resides today but most probably two years on it's been, everything that was in it, sold. When I started writing the manuscript, the first versions, it was probably still in storage somewhere awaiting dispatch, the stock, to other ice rinks.

Beyond answering many texts saying "Has the ice rink really closed?" and "What happened?" that's how my final departure went.

The end of the end had no particular date just that I recall standing on the ice and we'd done all we could. I realized I was leaving for the final time and said my goodbyes to Paul and Kevin and then to Lee and wished them all the best for the future and said how great it was that I'd gotten the chance to work with them and then left. I didn't shed a tear but I didn't want to leave. I recall talking to Lee for a while and then looking back at them all on the ice before I left. A sad way to end.

CHAPTER TWENTY ONE

Saturday 29th October 2016.

I've wrote two versions, alongside many versions of this manuscript, and would like to include both, for details sake, in this, the final version. Every time I write this manuscript, or re-write, I feel like I've always missed something or got something else to say but scrolling past and down the document recently upon this re-write I feel like I've finally hit the nail on the head and have a document in front of me that I can call, beside grammatical editing, finished and to be proud of. It's been a long path and I've no idea how long it's taken me to do this from start to finish but I'm glad that throughout I've stuck with it. Writing is a passion rather than a job so I've been doing this in my spare time amongst work, shopping and anything else. It's taken a back step for a long time until recently I discovered the manuscript again and re-wrote the first chapter and enjoyed it. I felt like I'd finally found a rhythm and you have that version in front of you now. Thanks for sticking with it and making it all worthwhile.

The first edition:

2015.

More than a year on and The Leisurebox still stands. The last time I went past the empty shell of 73-75 Pershore Street I was riding my motorbike only a couple of weeks ago. I stopped off at the old stomping ground The Dragon Inn that I, Siraj, Iqbal, Sean, Kassum and Rory alongside countless others used to visit so often and as a result got recognised by one of the bar staff. The chef I remember and a couple of the waiters. In general people don't stick around at The Dragon Inn because it's that kind of job, not one that many enjoy.

The last time I'd encounter the building, on written record, while it was standing.

To my understanding the land that The Leisurebox stands on will be flattened and upon it will be built flats. I've seen a proposal picture and it has a green, benches, a communal area and so on it looks like it's trying to create a resident feel. In my opinion it's more ridiculously expensive housing for posh clients in the remains of what I've always said should have been a grade listed building. Birmingham city council have a habit of destroying the city's finest buildings in order to replace it with modern works so it's of little surprise in truth.

In consideration that the old shell is still standing more than a year after closure I fear it could be a while before Birmingham can make a decision on if destroying and old classic was really worth it just to make way for the experiment of today's day and age, time will tell.

The second, this, edition:

As per the above date at start of chapter.

In truth I've just re-wrote the above and shortened it down to include what was needed otherwise you'd be reading the same thing twice for no good reason. Well, what can I correct given that another year, and almost two, has passed?

The buildings been demolished and workmen have been digging it up for an age. One small something remains at the back of the building but is too far out the way to figure out what it is. I've no idea if they've dug the basement up or left it but the ground looks to hollow to me to be all the way down to the bottom of the basement. Might make for an interesting dig for future archaeologists. I'd like to think the Planet Ice sign and flooded rooms still remain hidden. I smile at the idea that a part of it survived.

I said somewhere around the end of my 18th birthday chapter that I was, at some point, going to include more about Sophie but I'd like to correct that. Well, I am but not in the way that I might have when I wrote that. You see Sophie was someone that I liked but she liked someone else. I got involved and tried to make sure that she knew that he wasn't right for her and that she'd been mistreated but she never viewed it that way and took a long time until she did and moved on. I got way too involved and recall one occasion that the other party, the lad, pulled me into the first aid room to ask what I'd done and why. I was somewhat surprised that we had an adult conversation instead of getting a beating but the point of writing this is that any trouble or headache that I went through was mostly because I couldn't, or wouldn't, let go and therefore it only prolonged the entire episode. Some people you just never understand and I guess she was someone I'd tried to but failed and probably hadn't lived enough to understand that giving up trying to, understand that is, was the better option.

The Sashi episode is what it is. Anything I needed to say has been written in the appropriate chapter. At the risk of sounding like a broken record we haven't talked or seen one another in a long time. A more detailed account of her story can be read in my other work *C is for Cancer - A Memoir*. I'd like anyone who forms an opinion on what I've wrote to realise that my account is only one side to a difficult story to tell.

I phoned the job centre during the final weeks I spent at The Leisurebox and signed on not long after. I got a job after not very long and have been there ever since. The advisor said I had the best job searching record he'd seen in a while. I made good friends, but haven't seen since, another advisor that worked there. The job centres a horrid place that put the fear of god in me. I particularly hated the once a week session they made you go to, otherwise they'd stop your benefit money.

If you visit The Leisurebox's page on Facebook and click on photos and then in the albums click timeline photos and keep scrolling down until you reach the onesie party photos I'm in the thirteenth picture wearing a blue top with echo written on in white writing. The picture has three girls as the main subject but you can see me looking sidewards mid conversation in the background legs extended out. In the twelfth photo is Elijah. In the fourteenth is Elijah, Manish and JB and Steph is located in the nineteenth one. There's also three videos on that page and if you click on the one where everyone's in a line dancing you'll see me skate in, for a brief second, towards the end wearing the same blue echo top.

I'm glad my brother got to ice skate at least once at The Leisurebox although I doubt he'll remember it as he gets older. The video on the Facebook page of the family fun day of Manish is when he, my sister and mother attended. I purchased a toy car from the gift stand for him and they skated upstairs while I worked. I visited and said hello but left them to it. A special memory.

I dare to say that's all she wrote.

CHAPTER TWENTY TWO

A combination of The Leisurebox staff and security guards that I worked alongside between May 4th 2013 - May 6th 2013.

Rink Managers

Manish
Karen
Colin

Manager

Lee
Andy
Kevin

Bowling Technicians

Paul
Carl Lawrence
Josh
Matt

Accountants

Ruth
Jade
Connall

Receptionists

Nathan
Stephanie Lawrence
Cherelle

Jodie
Kirsty
Naomi

Regular Staff

Iqbal
Big J
Jermelle Banner
Jamz
Dan Bridgewater
Sean
Siraj
Rory
Karen Yates
Carl Yates
Aaron Daley
Aaron Averall
Natalie
Raffina
Lizz
Shiv
Shenila
Emma
Liam
Steph
Jimmy

Guards

Rob
Pete
Angie
LJ
Tony
Steven

I would like to clarify two things. (1) while the above names only appear under one section different people had different roles throughout my stay (2) not all of the above names worked at the rink all at the same time right up until the end.

(1) Just before we closed Raffina and Carl Yates were appointed, with no extra pay, supervisors of Bowling and Skate Hire. Shortly being so short that they never actually, to my memory, got to work an entire week in their new roles. The reason for receiving no extra pay was because the company, apparently, had not a single penny to spare to add onto our pay packets. This would be the first and last time while the building operated as The Leisurebox that there would be supervisors of Bowling and Skate Hire for before this point in time it had been the managers that had done the rotas and the rest looked after itself.

a. Josh and Carl Lawrence where our in-house DJ's not long after Roo, of whom was the DJ back in 2012, was sacked or left, I don't recall which. I recall Karen, the rink manager, not approving of certain type of music being played and thus I think stopped Carl Lawrence from being a DJ for a short period of time. Then again Karen was so out of touch with anything and everything I should add that we, as customers, quite enjoyed many a Friday night session under Carl thank you very much. Plus the party continued post Leisurebox when Colin was briefly rink manager at Peterborough and I and Carl used to make the trip once a week every weekend, for a short period of time, from Birmingham to Peterborough and back although that did mostly break Carl's engine in the car and thus it didn't really last long.

b. Connal did the accounting for one period of time but mainly worked in skate hire.

(2) Karen Yates, of whom was a cleaner, would leave long before we closed but nevertheless I worked alongside at one point. Equally: Jimmy, Emma, Jade, Shenila, Lizz and Dan had also left the company. Well, Dan never actually left rather never actually worked since he was a floater and had his own company and therefore after one of the summers never returned. Jimmy didn't stay very long at all and was the cousin of Andy. Emma left to return to her university course. Shenila was a floater and also at university when we closed. Jade returned when we shut to find a job with us but clearly it wasn't exactly the right time to do so.

Lizz left for another bowling company.

Part Three

The Small Memories

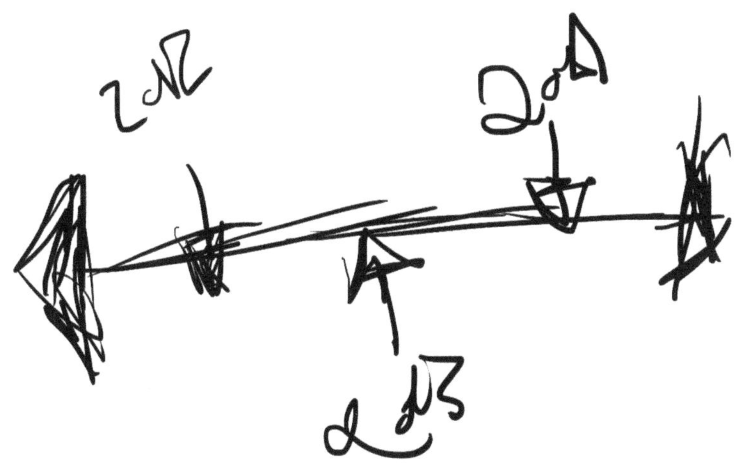

SMALL MEMORIES

1 - Mini Introduction

I've been writing *Part Two – The Story* for such a long time that it seems counter-productive to the main narrative of this story to add chapters to a story where chapters do not need to be added. This, therefore, is an extra addition whereby all the smaller memories can be included without fear of having perhaps a one or two line chapter as well as being free flowing in their own order rather than attempting to consult an ever changing diary of notes to keep the main narrative as accurate as possible.

SMALL MEMORIES
2 - The Rory Era

Google defines era as a long distinct period of history. Google also defines distinct as recognizably different in nature from something else of a similar type. I'd call that an accurate way to describe Rory. In short: unique, different and an individual with a unique talent for being around since forever with no one really knowing how he was found.

Rory, what a man. Well, if he was a man or not is debatable but I'll leave that down to someone other than myself to decide. The truth would be that Rory, if he liked it or not, would learn to grow very thick skin and put up with endless amounts of both physical and verbal abuse for he, thanks to Sean, I and many others was to fast become the punching bag of the group. Sometimes literally and others not.

I paint a negative picture and one that might have you wanting to pick up the phone and dial 101 meanwhile giving them all my information but allow to me to relax you somewhat in that the reality is not really as negative or as abusive as the above sounds. Fact is Rory gave us back as good as he got in both areas. Often I'd say the reason we gave him either verbal or physical abuse is because he'd only egg us on, inadvertent or not, and thus cause us to continue our abuse.

Did I mention we liked abusing Rory?

The memory that sticks out first on the list in regards to Rory (as I'm consulting an entire listen of handwritten notes in a lined notebook that I've been adding to throughout the entire time I've been writing *Part One - The Story* of this book) is the time that: I, Sean, Paul and Rory was present in the separate downstairs office that resided beside the clock in machine down a small set of stairs that at the top was a door that led out to the reception area.

The office only had one door to get in and out and a huge window that exposed it and all its contents to the entire landing and stairs area. Not very private indeed.

I can't really recall how or what happened besides Rory was in for another one of Sean's beatings and as a result would end up in the corner, on the floor, of yet another room. Paul called time and we all departed. Rory lived to fight another day meanwhile throwing verbal abuse in Sean's direction, again.

The next memory could spark writing about multiple memories. The time that someone of whom I can't recall, possibly I or Sean would hide Rory's clothes behind a wooden door that resided in the staff room. The staff room was located not on the main floors of the building but rather out of the way on it's own landing area and floor that was accessible via a set of stairs that resided just around the corner from the little office described in the last paragraph. Walking up one set of stairs and the first and only door on your left you'd enter into a decently sized room that had a flat wooden table and some chairs on the opposite side of the room. It would be common to often find either Kassum's hockey bag and kit or Rory's clothes on the seats with no sign of anyone else ever being in this room. It wasn't a room that was widely used if ever and really was out of the way. We called it the staff room because it was just a name it was given.

In relation to Rory's clothes there was a flat surfaced area that we could climb up on top of and sit on. High up. Imagine it if you will as the height of a wardrobe (but taller) and you'd climb up the wall hoisting yourself up to sit on top of it. It wasn't a wardrobe, that's just a literal comparison to enable to gain a mental image. At the end of this area was a wooden door that was more of a small square and was part of the wall. I don't really recall what was behind this door besides possibly some pipes, I didn't really like the look of the grubby darkness so decided never to take a look. Rory being Rory used to leave his clothes on top of this area and so I or Sean when we found them on rare occasions would hide them and his shoes behind this door so that (and we never did get to see his reaction) would be unable to find them. Common to say that we'd often have to tell him where we'd hid his clothes so that we could go home and lock up the building as he spent quite a while looking.

And that was Rory.

Also worthwhile including, since we're in the staff room, is the singular heel that once a female lost after sexual intercourse, I think. It's safe to say that the 1970's wasn't the only time period in this building that rumours of staff enjoying one another a little too much would surface. It seems many only had the confidence, or wanted to, say such rumours to me once the building had closed. Skate hire, or the back of, was subject to a fair few sexual sessions also, or so I'm told. Still, no chance of you being one of those, ey Rory?

SMALL MEMORIES
3 - Outside The Comfort Zone

Summer. Summer was an enjoyable period at The Leisurebox due to both the nature of the business as well as the location. Located on Pershore Street it was only a stone's throw away from many key areas of the city centre. A five minute walk to The Dragon Inn, our regular watering hole. A further five minute walk in the opposite direction to the Bullring. In business terms it was a pleasure because coming out of, on the rare days this happened, baking sun and into a very cold ice rink to partake in whatever you felt like doing on that given day was just a joy. Not having to pay for the privilege, as staff you didn't have to pay to enter, bowl or skate, was what made it for I and other staff all the more enjoyable. I'd say that during any given summer the rink was also a place where people suddenly became more happy and therefore we'd often spend more time standing around talking post shift or around the corner at The Dragon Inn wasting away hour after hour.

Outside of the rink summer also marked the point whereby we as staff would go clothes shopping. Sean had a collection of Hi Top Nike's purchased from the JD outside the bullring and the JD on the bottom floor of the Bullring, in kids sizes, and well to this day I'm still rocking the same pair of Hi Top's that I purchased from the JD outside the Bullring for £60-75 approx. all that time ago. I should probably change them but these days I spend more time wearing my motorbike boots (RST Trachtech Evo WP) than I do anything else so is a kind of redundant purchase truth be told, to me at least.

Photography was also a joy during this time because, while I had it and it was sunny, I'd often spend my time walking over the canals and then return to leave the camera in the locker while I skated and commute home after a hard days, cough, work. I do miss that I don't have the luxury of being in the city centre to just walk out and take photos anymore. Any city centre, I'd imagine, is prime location to have a place to reside and set of from in-between shots. The base that gets you to any location and saves you time in terms of transportation. Probably why I gave up on photography for so long, but not all together, after we shut. Photography of ice hockey at the rink wasn't all that glamorous because I didn't have the knowledge or equipment to shoot all that well in low light. My best glass was something like F 3.5, the kit lens, or something. I did latter get a 70-300mm Tamron but even that had high F stops and therefore wasn't great. Still what was not so good to be was appreciated by those around me a little more. I still like shooting action now but prefer outdoor action on sunny day's with the sky as a backdrop. The UEC BMX 2014 Birmingham Championship being a prime example, the best day, beside the sun burn, I've ever had. Slightly off topic here but that sun burn, shooting that event on that weekend, was almost the reason I didn't go to the interview for M&S on the Monday afterwards. Thankfully I did and now, two and a bit years on, I'm still with them.

The first summer, so the summer of 2013 under Manish, was an enjoyable time but also came with some uncomfortable moments. Flyering was very much one of them if not the core memory of this uncomfortable side of such an enjoyable period of time.

At that time and more than likely still remain today is not naturally part of my characteristics to want to engage with the people that stop you and attempt to bombard you with details of their charity and take your details let alone become one of them. Ok, flyering wasn't that extensive but seemed somewhat familiar and therefore I attempted to do everything I could to avoid it. The aim of flyering was to hand out leaflets to people waking past and get them to want to visit our ice rink to boost business. A relatively easy and ok job for someone that enjoys that line of work but I didn't.

Upon reflection there are worse things to be doing than walking the streets in the baking sun while getting paid unsupervised with your friends in the city centre.

There are some confessions to be made as to how I overcome a large part of time during this period but there is little to no damage to be done in revealing such truths of that time since it was so long ago so I don't hesitate to hold back details.

The day combined of three main memories.

Firstly standing outside of The Leisurebox itself with I, Sean and Sean's friend John.

Secondly to walk around town with Kassum and Steph.

Third and final is walking around town with just Sean.

As I departed or became separated form Kassum and Steph and instead wondered around with Sean it became apparent that I was not going to shift a huge amount of these flyers any time soon and therefore boarded any bus with Sean and would dump the flyers in the blue tray that you find at the front of the bus with the newspapers in. I recall doing this exactly once but basically dumping everything I had, and that was that.

Meanwhile Kassum and Steph enjoyed a pub of their choosing. Not something I'd have risked myself at the time but I was always straight to the point and very by the book.

Nathan Denny

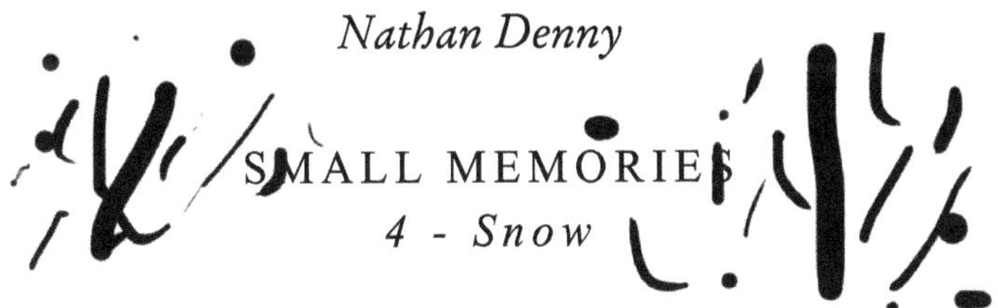

SMALL MEMORIES
4 - Snow

All I recall is that one day sitting at home rather bored and having nothing to do, possibly still a steward at this point, I saw a video on Facebook posted by Jamz and JB skating around an empty rink performing tricks. I left home and boarded the bus into town and by the time I arrived the shutters at the front of the rink where just being shut and locked. As Kevin, Andy and possibly others turned around and we exchanged some words and I'd had a wasted trip. They got in their warm cars while I turned around to realize that the buses had stopped running. I didn't really think about it at the time because I'd never rode or driven at that point but it was clearly due to a combination of weather and road conditions.

With the buses stopped I was faced with a walk from Pershore Street into and beyond Tyseley. I recall being one or two miles away from home when the first bus that I could have caught passed me. I considered that a win in consideration standing around in the cold not knowing when the buses would get going again would have been counter-productive and would have seemed like a very, very long time.

You're only young once. Never again.

SMALL MEMORIES
5 - Trapped

Raffina once revealed her very unique and rare party trick.

The party trick was her very unique ability to walk over to, and get her foot stuck in, the drain that the water and leftover ice was dumped on top of once the Zamboni (the more technical people will correct me on the actual name of the machine) had finished cutting the ice and was making its way to be parked in the garage area.

I think her shoe got the worst of it. With a fresh pair of the finest Leisurebox grey thick socks on she took a pair of bowling shoes and made her way home with a new pair of footwear to add to her collection. Spraying them several times over before putting them on and loathing have to do so in the process.

Neither she nor anyone else repeated that accident since. Thankfully.

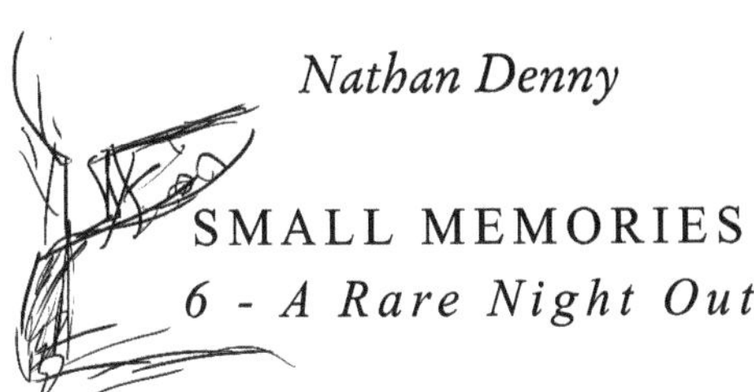

Nathan Denny

SMALL MEMORIES
6 - A Rare Night Out

A proper night out that is. A night out to us, or at least mostly to I, Sean, Iqbal and a fair few of the others for the majority of our time at The Leisurebox was spent at The Dragon Inn enjoying our drinks quietly at a table while we observed the much more energetic fellow pub goers downing their pints dressed for a night out at the nearby nightclubs. On this very rare occasion it was our turn. Broad Street.

It came about out of nowhere and somehow I, Sean, Kassum and Carl, that's Carl that lives local, the DJ, found ourselves driving around with Carl as the taxi driver one by one visiting each other's houses and getting ready and dressed for a night out on the town. I think it came about because Richard had suggested that we should go out, and so in the spare of the moment we did. Richard's someone of whom works at Solihull Ice Rink, was Blue Ice back then but is now under Silverblades ownership.

Carl drove us round to each of our houses with mine being last. I apparently took the most time to get ready. We all had alcohol in our system, beside Carl being the driver of course.

I was always rubbish at ironing shirts. I had all three of the guys come into my house instead of waiting outside in the car. Attempting to get two tipsy-ish lads to be quiet and not wake everyone asleep upstairs thankfully went to plan. Furthermore I asked both Sean and Kassum to iron my shirt in consideration they thought that they could do a better job, they couldn't. Beside criticizing my attempts to remove all creases, I failed horribly, they managed to do nothing but extend the time it took me to get ready and also fail in the process.

We finally made it to Broad Street in the early hours of the morning and met Kayleigh and Richard outside one of the main clubs on the strip, so to speak, it's lightly written, and made our way inside. You have to pay for the privilege of making your way inside the club to spend yet more money on drinks, something I despised and something Sean thought that he could avoid. I didn't pay for him. You knew full well what you were getting yourself into and yet didn't bring sufficient funds, not my problem. I've always been tight with my money, I call it sensible. Damage limitation. I think Kassum paid for him in the end.

That would also be the night that Kayleigh decided to test the strength of Kassum's boots by standing on them and possibly in heels. Kassum later explained many times over and it became an ongoing joke between ourselves that it hurt somewhat. No one knew why she thought it was a good idea. I'm sure Kassum could have otherwise proved his boots wasn't steel toe caps.

Beside the group latter making fun of my inability to dance and just standing on the dance floor bopping my head I think all went rather well. I tried, dancing isn't my thing at all. Then again neither are nightclubs.

If I recall correctly and a true rare occasion and not one I wish to nor have taken part in since was residing in a, well, a strip club? A lap dance club? I don't know what you'd formally call it, as far as formal goes in places such as those.

A tip I'd give to anyone if you find yourself in one of these places is never pull out a note of cash, even just £1, if you want a bit of peace. Sat at the bar I withdrew the money from the back of my phone to buy myself a drink and had a girl approach me "Would you like a dance?" I declined.

I think we all made fun of each other every time a girl attempted to get business of us since this wasn't something we'd done before or do since so was unique in that way. Seeing how we all reacted and picking out moments to use as abuse towards that person when it arose. I think Kassum gave Sean the worst time because he seemed somewhat flustered at times.

The entire reason we were inside is because Richard knew either the bouncers or the owners. I dread to think what we all looked like sitting inside but I couldn't wait to get out. Never again.

SMALL MEMORIES
7 - Photography

One of the events that I attended was a Jamaican music festival hosted just outside of the or around the corner from the art museum.

There's little to be said other than the time when a male approached me with a leaflet in his hand and asked me to take a photograph of it and promote it on wherever my pictures would end. He wasn't hard pressing in the matter and didn't ask me to literally take one in person, I didn't, but rather an overall very friendly experience.

SickBeNurished.org

And that's my job done. Promise delivered at long last.

SMALL MEMORIES
8 - Eat Your Heart Out

Ming Moon. Located just a five minute walk away, as every location I've listed during this writing session seems to be, was an all you can eat buffet style building that some of us would visit for no reason other than we fancied eating our heart outs at somewhere other than The Dragon Inn. As much as I like my scampi and chips "Oh, that all be me please" in a very deep voice as Kassum would mock me many times over for as the waiter, whoever that may be on that given day, would approach me and ask who ordered the scamp and chips.

In truth Ming Moon was a bit of a con. Firstly because it was expensive, or so I seem to recall memories of standing at the card machine having had a mini heart attack as they informed us how much it all cost and secondly because it's a known fact that all you can eat style places are never really all you can eat because your mind tricks you and you end up eating perhaps less than what you'd eat out of just a regular meal anywhere else. Well, in my case at the very least since I can eat but I binge eat all the wrong foods rather than the right ones.

Mainly all the food at Ming Moon was covered in grease and was the fast food type rather than anything filling and good for you. I seem to recall sticking to three things; Chips, Chicken nuggets and ice cream. Unlimited refill on the ice cream was a blessing that revealed my inner child. Also made me rather bloated and to feel sick after a couple of dishes. I learnt after a couple of visits to pace out my time between dishes of ice cream with chatter and then I'd get more for my money. Places like Ming Moon never had a time limit on how long you could stay so you get away with being there as long as you liked.

Another fast food company and one that was located over the road from Ming Moon was Dixy Chicken.

Dixy was another place that meanwhile I never ate from, I don't like their food and towards the end of my time at The Leisurebox decided fast food was a no go if not in moderation, but spent a fair few visits to for the security guards or fellow staff members when passing that way. I'd never really go past it unless I had to in honesty but since everything was so close together it wasn't really a pain to go out my way for another five minute walk to get someone else food for them. I'd do it for the security guards because as you'd expect they couldn't leave their post or for fellow staff if I was having a break and they wanted something to eat. You didn't have to have a break at The Leisurebox to eat. I often sat in the skate hire eating my lunch while working in slow one thing after another to last me through my shift. Almost anything went, I'm sure you've gathered, at the rink, within reason.

SMALL MEMORIES
9 - Shopping With JB

The Leisurebox wasn't really a lucrative business and in truth probably lost more money than it gained, another possibility for its closure, and so that meant that we, as staff, only picked up twopence once a month in our pay packets. Being young with very little outgoings meant that beside the money we spent at The Dragon Inn one of the many other ways to spend it was in clothes shops. We spent nearly every day of the week at the place that some people would only come to once a week and dress their best so we had to keep our wardrobes up to date and look fashionable when for when the weekend arrived. Well, also for the many outings that we attended in the local area and so on. Shopping wasn't really anything special but one of the more different periods in time was when I and JB joined forces and shopped together. Bit of a weird time in truth because despite the fact we'd done things together in groups we'd never really bonded with just I and him. I guess you'd have to be anyone but I and JB and around at the time to understand why it was a little questionable that us two had gone out to do something social on our own. Raffina questioned it and I imagine others might not have understood it either. We used to visit places like: JD, Burton's, Primark and whatever else existed at the time and had clothes within our budget. JD's was JB's shop because he liked anything that was made by Nike and grey or blue or a combination of both. Burton's I liked but was a little on the more upmarket side and only ever purchased from their maybe once or twice. Primark was a mash up of getting budget clothes that would do for a weekend or two and then reside in the back of the wardrobe. Some bargains to be had if you could find something you liked but their stock depth and range was and has always been poor. We spent the rest of our time walking around shops window shopping. JD's had a good selection of trainers but on the expensive side. Sean used to buy pairs of shoes like once every week or couple of weeks that cost approx £60-70 a pair. I never understood it but its how he wanted to splash the cash. A collection of Nike's if he's still got them. Then again shoes are always cheaper in Junior sizes. I don't really recall how I and JB's adventures came about nor how they ended but there we are. I purchased a printed sweatshirt from River Island the once and haven't recovered financially since. Lord only knows what possessed me to pay their prices.

SMALL MEMORIES
10 - The Unhappy Birthday

Iqbal. The only person that when my birthday happened on May 25th 2014 would turn up to meet me at The Dragon Inn and bother doing something, anything, with me on a social level. I think Rory might have turned up also, in fact yes he did because we ended up at his pub, if not a little boring was something better than nothing.

Iqbal also had along with him for company his cousin. Similar to my age if not a year or two older or younger, I never could tell on that night, and in the end made for good company. I haven't spoken to the lad since but did follow him on Instagram once, I think he's closed the account or hasn't posted since.

Iqbal said something along the lines of "You find out who your true friends are in times like this." You could view it as someone who was in the right place at the right time painting a bad picture of everyone else, or, you could take the view that I did and do this day that it as true as it gets.

The situation was that we'd just lost our jobs and yet no one would bother to come out or do anything so the day basically fell flat on its face and it was more about spending time with those that we'd spent a fair few years of our lives with working alongside up to that point rather than having loads of money to splash out. Iqbal, despite just losing his job, was always the first to put his hand in his pocket and offer to buy someone a drink. A constant theme throughout knowing Iqbal even when he had a job together.

We stood in the equivalent of a beer garden to get some fresh air and went back into a small back almost private room, a room with a TV that no one used rather than being private. Rory knew the pub owner and therefore we just relaxed watching football. I wanted to go to the Saint Patrick's Day parade (upon editorial I've noted this as incorrect and was more than likely the annual Birmingham Pride area hosted with fares, music stages and drink in the gay quarter literally down the road from The Dragon Inn, it requires an arm band to enter and is heavily, heavily guarded) but meanwhile Iqbal was up for it the entry fee was high and the pennies counted. I think we spent a large part of that day standing around wondering and looking for things to do both at The Dragon Inn and finally at Rory's pub but inevitably never wondered much further than either of them.

So, meanwhile I did see people after that day from the rink thankyou Iqbal, Rory and Iqbal's cousin/s. Yes there was one further cousin but we didn't really talk.

SMALL MEMORIES
11 - Recapping The Knowns

A possible recap of the already known parts of this story. My notes say one thing but my memory recalls writing another. Again there's been so many versions of the main part of this story written over a period of time so long I can't recall when it began that I forget what I've included and what I haven't in the final version. I'll keep it light to save time in the event that it has somewhere been included and forgotten about. If vice versa than apologies for the limited details.

There are two knowns to recap.

The first known is at the time point in time we were working inside The Leisurebox after closure to help remove everything from inside I deemed myself to be on a budget and did two things to save money, both not entirely necessary but I knew what it was like to have to make money last over several months after the NCP episode and didn't want a repeat here after all we'd just had Natalie's christening, Steph's birthday and a few other outings prior to closure so had spent a bit more money than what I would of liked to, of course all that money was spent in the hope of earning it back and without a second thought that I might not but where money could be saved in this situation I did. The first thing I did was to commute via bicycle. The second was to save money on food where money could be saved. The food one really was the extreme out of the two. I enjoyed riding a bicycle and it made a nice change to be out in the fresh air and feel free with the wind through my hair.. no, I'll stop that. I like cycling from time to time.

So, food. At first it started out with eating the tortillas, and I write that lightly, that had been left in the machine prior to closure with the intent to sell to customers but now had been left in a machine turned off as the kitchen, if I recall correctly, was one of the first things to be emptied out. The tortillas, and thankfully for me, inadvertently, had been left inside for the entirety of removal. The extreme with the food was that I'd end up eating the tortillas until there was no more to be eaten and they almost certainly had gone past being stale. I filled a plastic cup, the ones intended to be used to be filled with drinks for customers, stewards, staff etc during operation but know laid empty, gathering dust and looking sorry for themselves next to an non-operational drinks machine, full to the brim with tortillas and deemed that my portion of food for that given break or time out between working.

The less extreme and note that I'm referring to is the time that while the rest of the staff purchased bags of chips from the local chippy just a, you guessed it, five minute walk away near the outdoor markets and meals from Dixy chicken I instead popped into Tesco and purchased a bag of tortillas that cost less than £1 and lasted me a few days. I walked down the street with the group as they made their way towards Dixy and had a bag in my hand munching on a tortilla as if the world had ended and poverty had settled in meanwhile office workers standing on their fag breaks outside the bottom floor doors leading onto the street I was walking on started and looked startled like I was an alien from another planet. Birmingham's full of characters and I was just playing my part.

The second known was the tour around the building that Andy had given I and Steph not long after we started working for the company. The small hatch that led down a small set of steps into a dark unlit room that had only the hatch as an in and out method and a tour of the upstairs that neither I nor, I believe Steph, knew about until we where shown it existed. I'll leave it there with that one as the whole Andy and hatch episode sound very familiar. Well, to me at least.

SMALL MEMORIES
12 - Upstairs

On a related note, and to carry on talking about the third floor, the very top floor of the building it would be appropriate to mention the time that I, Sean and Siraj used the top floor of the building to play hide and seek. There's two warnings before you begin to carry on reading. Firstly is that if I've written this in the main narrative then please do skip this chapter as it's just an entire repeat and secondly would be that if you're six foot or over like myself then hide and seek is not a game you should attempt to play when it comes to the hiding part because it's near impossible. As I was just about to find out.

PS: If you're six foot and ginger furthermore add this to the reasons as not to attempt to hide.

My turn came to hide. As I've mentioned before I was very to the rulebook and playing around with hide and seek seemed like the worst thing in the world I could do. A thousand questions buzzed around my head as I asked myself; "What if a manger walked upstairs know? What happens if I get caught? Is this all worth it?" I proceeded to bite the apple from the tree and take the risk. I didn't get caught thankfully. Well, I did, but just not by a manger and instead by Siraj as they walked past me and said they had seen my bright orange hair bobbing around above the boxes and had walked past me momentarily to make me think I hadn't been seen. I'd be no good in where's wally I tell you.

Siraj found a good hiding place. The location wasn't one that I'd noticed before he had hidden there and one that I questioned why it existed. My father used to tell me as a youngster to "Look up, all the details at the top of buildings, all these people walk past day by day and never know what they're missing." I paint a man of interest but there's not one it's more an observation. Back to the present with Siraj he had hidden on a, and again how do I describe this, a little wooden walkway with a banister in front of it blocking it. Envision if you will a wall, a blank wall in front of you and you're standing in front of it looking at it but from a short distance away. To the left is another wall and to the right another wall. You're basically looking at any given part of a room but in a much smaller space and with no doors either side. The wooden banister would then join the entire thing together. I don't have a picture sadly. The walls showed no signs of ever having doors nor being any but doors. A strange design and one I never did figure out nor ask about. My only theory was that as there was an old DJ area and a salsa bar upstairs within visual distance it must have been a place that people climbed up to and danced on, females, like dancing girls in that club I unfortunately found myself in with the group on Broad Street. only smaller, in the 70's/80's and a little more class. I liked to think of it that way at least.

SMALL MEMORIES
13 - The Final Third

A small inner note of saddening passes within me as I recall for the final time a brief note on the upstairs, the third floor to be exact, of the building.

The first out of two final notes is the time that I moved all the skates that had been dumped into skate hire from another ice rink and I took it upon myself to clean them up walking the full length from skate hire to a large open space in the third floor a handful at a time until they were all gone. At the top of the stairs on the far side I took the following path; right into the DJ and Salsa bar area, left through a door and then on your immediate left. Right next to, and or in line with, the room that had the DJ speakers that sat above the ice rink in. If you see old photographs and sketches of the ice rink from the 70's under The Silverblades you'll see the room poking out like a little square box in the corner of the upper section of the ice.

The second final note is all of the chairs, gym equipment and anything and everything had had been left lying about on the top floor. I always walked past and said every time should a fire break out that would be the end of the place. It could have been once upon a time when the actual fire happened. In a way it was the end of the place. I guess only now am I putting two and two together in a different kind of way.

SMALL MEMORIES
14 - All Fun And Games

A portion of time has passed since I penned the last chapter and therefore need to adjust slightly. Ah, I see. Teddies, softly softly.

One of the perks, amongst many, about working at The Leisurebox was in its entirety the single handed head start that we had over the public in attempting to win the teddies that where placed inside the arcade machines. We'd wait until the man had visited, the man being the one who worked for the company that owned the machines and whom the owners of the rink had rented them from, and filled them up and then spend all our spare change picking out the easiest ones and making a collection. Personally I didn't get all that many, two I think my household still retains. Sooty and an unknown other.

While we're on the note of fun and games I could recall the time that JB alerted us all, rather quietly on the down low, shh shh might I add, to the fact that the pool table in the bar area was broken and you could literally remove the section that the balls where held in and take them out for free. For a period of time we removed it entirely and then put it under the table and just let the balls roll into the empty wooden area and refill the triangle when we wanted another game. Naturally it has to be added that the managers didn't very much like this and stopped us from using it once discovered. I think we had a game of hide and seek and occasionally managed the free game once in a blue moon up until the man, not him again, the big bad wolf in this one, came and "fixed it," bugger.

And while we're on the note of the bar area I could recall the endless amount of times that I purchase the KP Nuts, or just nuts in general, from the bar area while Aaron was working and end up dropping half of them on the floor while missing my mouth and leaving him with a clean up job after every visit. He got annoyed eventually and refused to sell them to me. I've discussed this since with him on a chance encounter at Solihull Ice Rink. Further apologies my fellow Ginge.

Have I mentioned the time Sean, Siraj and JB were suspended for throwing darts rather recklessly and ended up damaging the wall leaving loads of little holes in? I have now. It was always said it was a funny thing that Andy, the manager, did the same but never got suspended. No one got the sack in the end so no tears were shed. The darts incident was followed shortly by the knock-out shot to the wall on the stairs leaving a gaping hole in the wall. Big J didn't get sacked for that, but did get suspended I think, either.

SMALL MEMORIES
15 - Hidden Passages

The note reads "Smoking out the back," I'll modify to a short read regarding the back area.

I may have referred to the road that ran around the back of the building and joined up with the crossroads outside the building when it was under the name The Silverblades. I refer again to the road that, at present, does not connect but is met by a brick wall, a dead end. I'd love to be able to walk through the wall just like Rodney did in *Goodnight Sweetheart*. Well, it wasn't Rodney but that's who you'll know him as, you know, the one out of *Only fools and horses*.

The area out the back was nothing more than a slim alley way that had two doors either side. One made its way out to the front of the building and the other at the opposite end to this now dead end. A dead end that had nothing but illegally parked cars, dust bins and the homeless. There was the occasion that a group of kids or troubled looking individuals occupied the street when putting the bins out but I never got any bother.

This alley way pathed the way for many a warm summers day of conversation with a peering view through the fence that on the other side had the open space car park that joins with The Travelodge hotel. The alley way being overlooked by the high rise windows that had hotel rooms on the other side. I, Iqbal and a fellow female member of staff of whom had evaded my memory until moments ago once occupied the hotels inside area one Sunday morning shift when the building was closed and we were waiting for it to open. We, all three of us, should have gone home. We waited, sadly, and worked.

There's many a tale to tell. Well, not really. An area that staff smoked in during brakes or fag brakes and then went back inside to the mad house. There's nothing glamorous about it although it sketched in my memory as an area of freedom to speak your mind to your fellow co-worker before you resumed normality.

I recall a set of stairs that met the fire door leading out to the alley way. I recall one time a few went up into the very small landing area that for a moment if you forgot where you really were you could mistake it for an upstairs house landing area with the doors leading out of it being bedrooms. I never do recall what was inside. The landing was unlit and I didn't like the look of it. Another unique space that was hidden well away from view, this building had plenty and I loved to explore them all countless times. Just not this one.

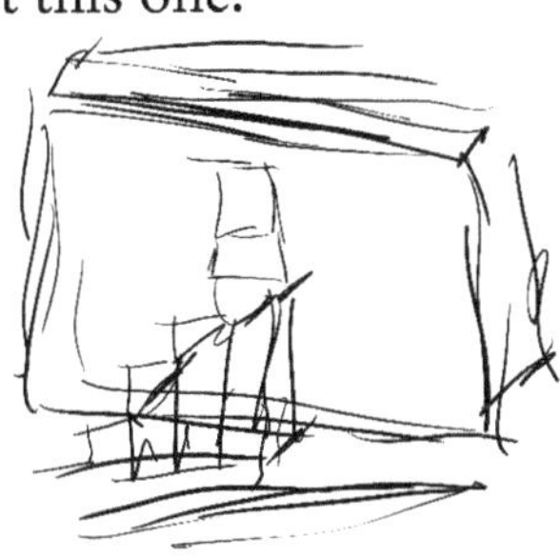

SMALL MEMORIES
16 - Luke

Luke had mysteriously left the story for an unknown reason but I had my special moment when eventually he returned.

The only thing that had changed when he did return was that I had got better at skating and made friends with just about everyone whereas he returned possibly worse than when he'd left and still didn't speak to anyone beside the female, Vicky, that he visited with.

We skated at The Leisurebox for a few weeks when he'd visit and then once it closed we moved onto Solihull Blue Ice and I became known for buying their 70p toast but that all soon faded out and we drifted apart once more.

70p for a couple of pieces of toast and some spreadable jam in a small pot, rip off merchants. Well, that's Solihull Blue Ice, now Silver Blades, for you.

Not to take away from Luke's chapter, or mini one at that, but if you're going to visit the ice rink in Solihull then I'd advise that you visit the website and register for an ice card, regardless of if you intend to return, beforehand and take the cash to pay, to get in, rather than pay with a card because they add, despite any other discounts, 50p to put your card into the machine and enter your pin. I also advise that you take a member with you of whom won't be skating because the lockers, small ones, cost 50p at a time and the big ones £1 and the money is non-refundable and you can only open the locker once, so basically once you open it you have to put another set of money in to lock it again. They, despite a guard, do not search your bags and therefore I'd hide away on the seating at the back and take your own, small, assortment of food because the cafe is overpriced like hell as are, as normal, the vending machines.

Mini travel guide to Solihull Ice Rink over.

Can you tell that while it's my only option to skate, locally, I'm not overly fond of the place?

SMALL MEMORIES
17 - Stop

I wrote somewhere in the main narrative that the story of how I learned to hockey and T stop was a story for another time. I wrote this in one version of the main manuscript that I fail to recall if it's the same one I could find at the top of this document and you at the start of the book. I never, however, in any of the narratives wrote the story, here it is.

I never did learn to T Stop and can only hockey stop twisting my feet counter clockwise to the left and not clockwise. I'd love to be able to hockey stop both ways but never managed to wrap my head around it despite Kassum attempting to teach me many times over.

I owe a thank you to Khy, Matt (&. Cracks?) and many other stewards of the classic era that spent the time, even a brief moment, attempting to teach me the basics allowing me to get my head around it much later on, just as Sashi had done with the whole "drag your foot behind you like this" tale many moons ago.

I may only do the same things over and over when skating but I'd pinpoint this as the period in time when they were learnt and every moment I've spent skating since has been fine tuning them during each and every session thus allowing me to make them look painstakingly easy. The movements are just sketched into your mind and your body becomes jelly as you make the minefield of fellow skaters nothing more than objects to manoeuvre around.

SMALL MEMORIES
18 - Local Comforts

"Just put the money in you'll be fine, honestly just try it it's fun" Bianca says as I insert a ten pound note into the casino machine in the hope that I might see event a penny of it again in winnings, I never do. I never gambled again after that.

Bianca was a friend of Raffina's that turned up occasionally and the gambling was done at the Genting casino located, you guessed it, a five minute walk around the corner opposite Dixy Chicken. Towards the end of our spell at The Leisurebox we bumped into Keith of whom used to work at the ice rink for security and now worked on the reception desk, was a nice reunion seeing a friendly face amidst all the personal chaos life had thrown in my path at the time.

Genting for me was the home of many a night spent with the lads. I have my membership card lying around gathering dust either in the cup downstairs or scattered somewhere under my TV stand area of my bedroom floor where it has remained since my last approximate visit in May of 2014. Well, I might have been since and probably did but I remember at the time they had a promotion on that if you visited for a certain amount of days in that month you'd get something free. You didn't have to pay to get in, as far as I recall. Well, not with a membership card at least at the time, but naturally it encouraged you to spend your money inside. For me personally as I've already cleared up I never gambled, or don't recall doing so, after than ten pound loss but did spend money in the restaurant area and bar while everyone else played the tables and enjoyed themselves.

I remember after the rink closed and Rory text me out the blue and organized for whoever out of the lads would turn up to watch the England game on the big TV in the casino. We sat in the bar area and watched. I think we spent most of the time cramming as many seats as close together as possible since everyone else was sitting in awkward areas and not really allowing us to relax. A good memory and day out regardless.

I recall further the time that we lost our jobs and visited the casino in one big group, I'd call that the last time most of us where together. Aaron bumped into someone that he knew who worked at the casino and informed him of all of our current situations and the worker responded with, something along the lines of, "Ah swear down you've all just lost your jobs and you're in here gambling away your money" as most of us laughed.

The restaurant was terrible, for me anyway. The first time I visited I took a photo of the cutlery and posted a photograph on social media asking what an earth it was and how I used it and the second occasion I ate next to nothing, as I had done on the first. Then you had the regulars that played some form of game with dominos at the bottom in their own private area bothering no one and asking inadvertently not to be bothered in return.

The upstairs small smoking area, complete with a red light that sparked many a late night deep in thought conversation between whoever I spent the time with up their between fag breaks and just to get some fresh air and escape from the main floor once and a while.

I'd call the casino the middle ground. The Dragon Inn was my place to be, I hated, and still do, nightclubs and I felt in the middle of comfortable and uncomfortable in the casino. I didn't really appreciate just lucky I was or the time we as a group where having amongst all this but I recall this memory with a smile. A genuine joy.

SMALL MEMORIES
19 - Claim To Fame

We all have a claim to fame and I feel the need to tell you mine. While personally I'd much rather tell you about the people of whom I held respect for and considered fame worthy instead, as modern society dictates, I'll tell you instead about the so called celebrities I once upon a time occupied the same building as.

Famous person number one was Tucker Jenkins from *Grange Hill*, or more formally and named at birth Todd Carter.

Skating in preparation for his, at the time, upcoming appearance on *Strictly Come Dancing*. Accompanied by: a male coach, a female coach and the TV crew, as I recall a singular camera man. The truth was that I doubt very much of the footage made it into the series because Todd, in my view, couldn't skate to save his own life. I didn't make a big thing of it back then and today retain the same sense of dullness for his presence. In simple terms we occupied the same building because I turned up for a shift and found him, in his own cordoned off area, at the top of the ice pad with the three aforementioned accomplices. Todd was a nice enough person mind so I shouldn't be too harsh. While I never spoke directly to Todd he, as far as I recall, said hello and goodbye, in a brief manor, to the managers each time he came and went, they're human after all. I think the most striking memory was watching his private car, and driver, pull up on the pavement outside the rink when it was time to leave, oh how the other half live.

Famous person number two was Joe Pasquale.

There's not much, if anything, to write because I wasn't actually in the building at the same time as him although was told by the managers each time he had been. That's all the excitement and gossip I've got. Well, I did say if anything, you were warned.

On a side note I do feel that while we weren't exactly in a state of closing soon at the time these so called famous people used the rink I do feel a little bit more, anything for that matter, could have been done in the way of a brief mention on Strictly to feature The Leisurebox to gain popularity. I can't help but feel the men with money used the place as they had seen fit and then upped and left without a real thank you, saving us. I won't ramble on too much because the truth is the owner wanted to sell the place, as I'm sure I've wrote, so it was set in stone anyhow. Still, would have been nice to see the workplace on the T.V.

SMALL MEMORIES

20 - That's All She Wrote

I'm tired. I'm tired physically, mentally and in every other way possible. I'm going to write up on two of the last three notes in my diary and I'm done, we're done, it's over.

> Note 1.

On the buildings second floor, the floor the ice rink was on, there was a hidden bar. You'd have to scratch your head to try and remember it if you didn't work there of course due to access restriction and lack of importance of the feature while the building operated. The bar had long been shut down and was located behind two double doors and blocked off by a big curved sheet of wood that was at the bottom of the ice rink, the skate hire end. I visited inside upon a couple of occasions and at first scared myself when I discovered the gigantic mirror that was to the immediate left as you walk through the double doors. The room, in truth, was a fire trap waiting to happen with all sorts of ice mats stored inside all the while blocking the path one was supposed to walk along. With the mats, and quite a few of them at that, stored one on top of another it would be fair game to think that if anywhere was going to go up, in a fireball like it had done some years before, you'd better not be anywhere near this area. The bar was grotty at best and all that resided inside covered in thick cobwebs. All the bar screamed in the modern day was mental video reels, in my head, of what once the activity that partook inside looked like for it had long since been vacant of any human activity.

> Note 2

The DJ booth was another unknown area of interest. Hidden in plain sight but long since, like the bar, vacant from any human activity. Once a spectacular room during the ice rinks hay day it had since, in the modern day, been left to lay vacant and become derelict. I'd say the condition was such that it was a health and safety risk to even walk inside and for that reason alone the furthest I got inside at the best of times was the three, maybe four, steps that lead inside the room. Dark, unlit, dinging and creepy it wasn't a desirable place to visit beside the first, maybe two, time/s I visited and discovered it.

I'm talking of course about the DJ booth that would have resided at the back of the stage in the 1970's approx. and not the modern, or more modern at least than the one I'm describing, DJ Booth that the people of whom had visited while the building operated as The Leisurebox would have known. Always hidden behind the big curtain not once was it revealed or seen by the public.

To access it required to walk through the current DJ Booth through a fire door and then down an alley way past the four, maybe five, large windows that resided at the side of the building and eventually you'd find it approximately three quarters of the way towards the end. Because of the nature of the location you often, or at least I remember doing so, had to radio to someone else and tell them where you were going. You had to do so because the pit, the one that the ice dumped into via the Zamboni once cut, resided, open, beside the alleyway at the end also. The pit, as I'm sure I've told you, ran deep down the entire route of the building and once you were in there was no escaping. In reality the doors should have always, when not in use, been shut but we never did.

At the end of the alley way, or walkway, was a first aid room long since un-used.

The other method of visiting this passage was through the bar area although I seem to recall that the ice rink had since been adapted to block of being able to walk through and therefore, at best, all you could do was look onwards to the first aid room. Behind the wall that separated and hid the bar from the ice rink, on the floor, was the ice pad, or rather what stretched out underneath the barriers and remained untouched, I assume, from the moment it was frozen upon being laid.

The
END

TYPEFACE'S USED

Garamond, Times new roman, Saki, Oldstyle italic, Nanami, Comfortaa, Parchment, Neuton cursive, Nordica, Chapaza italic, Aver, Antipasto, Arual.

(All font credit goes to their respective owner and are available to download from dafont.com)

ALSO BY NATHAN DENNY

C is for Cancer - A Memoir

PHOTOGRAPHS

Due to printing costs photographs have not been included in this volume and instead will be available to purchase at a later date separately.

ILLUSTRATIONS

All illustrations have been designed (by Nathan Denny) using a Intuos draw pen tablet small (2017).

www.ingramcontent.com/pod-product-compliance
Ingram Content Group UK Ltd.
Pitfield, Milton Keynes, MK11 3LW, UK
UKHW020224250726
13967UKWH00001B/182

9 781389 835896